Englisch lernen mit

Jeffery
Deaver
Murderous Affairs

Berlitz Publishing
München • New York • Singapur

Berlitz Englisch lernen mit Jeffery Deaver
Murderous Affairs

Vokabelerklärungen und Übungen: Sigrid Köhler
Layout: Ute Weber
Cover-Gestaltung: Dominik Lommer
Projektleitung: Eva Betz

© 2008 Berlitz Publishing, München
© 2003 Jeffery Deaver für die Kurzgeschichten
For Services Rendered, *Triangle* und *Without Jonathan*

Berlitz Publishing
Mies-van-der-Rohe-Straße 1
D-80807 München

Das Werk und seine Teile
sind urheberrechtlich geschützt.
Jede Verwertung in anderen als den gesetzlich
zugelassenen Fällen bedarf deshalb der
vorherigen schriftlichen Einwilligung des Verlags.

Berlitz ist eine beim U.S. Patent Office und
in anderen Ländern eingetragene Marke.
Marca Registrada.
Marke von Berlitz Investment Corporation lizenziert.

Satz: Franzis print & media Gmbh, München
Druck: CS-Druck Cornelsen Stürtz, Berlin
Bindung: Stein + Lehmann, Berlin
Printed in Germany
ISBN 978-3-468-79231-1

Inhalt

Vorwort	**5**
Triangle	**7**
For Services Rendered	**41**
Without Jonathan	**85**
Lösungen	**110**
Wörterverzeichnis	**124**

Lieber Krimi-Fan,

mit den spannenden Kurzkrimis von Jeffery Deaver halten Sie endlich ein Englischbuch in der Hand, das Sie garantiert nicht mehr weglegen wollen. Und vor lauter Nervenkitzel merken Sie vielleicht gar nicht, dass Sie ganz nebenbei auch Ihre Englischkenntnisse gehörig auffrischen und erweitern.

Damit Ihr Lesevergnügen nicht durch das Nachschlagen unbekannter Wörter gemindert wird, sind die schwierigsten Vokabeln im Text blau markiert und in der Marginalspalte übersetzt. Interessante Wörter, die in einer Infobox erklärt werden, sind zusätzlich mit einem Sternchen gekennzeichnet. Alle übersetzten Wörter sind außerdem im Wörterverzeichnis im Anhang zusammengefasst.

Allein beim Schmökern in den Krimis können Sie sehr viel dazulernen. Vielleicht möchten Sie aber auch Ihr Grammatikwissen und Ihre Vokabelkenntnisse zusätzlich erweitern oder aber Ihr Textverständnis prüfen. Zu diesem Zweck finden Sie auf jeder Seite knifflige und unterhaltsame Übungen. Die Vokabeln aus dem Text werden dort noch einmal verwendet und bleiben dadurch viel besser im Gedächtnis haften – so können Sie später leichter darauf zurückgreifen. Selbstverständlich sind auch die Lösungen zu allen Übungen im Anhang abgedruckt.

Und nun wünschen wir Ihnen viel Spaß und Spannung beim Lesen!

Ihre Berlitz-Redaktion

Triangle

'Maybe I'll go to Baltimore.'

'You mean …' She looked over at him.

'Next weekend. When you're having the shower* for Christie.'   Party

'To see …'

'Doug,' he answered.

'Really?' Mo Anderson looked carefully at her fingernails, which she was painting bright red. He didn't like the color but he didn't say anything about it. She continued. 'A bunch of women 'round here – boring.   Haufen
You'd enjoy yourself in Maryland. It'll be fun,' she said.

'I think so too,' Pete Anderson said. He sat across from Mo on the front porch of their split-level house in sub-   Veranda •
urban Westchester County. The month was June and   mit versetzten
the air was thick with the smell of the jasmine that Mo   Geschossen

---

In den USA ist es üblich, eine Geschenkparty (shower, wörtlich   **info**
Dusche) zu veranstalten, wenn eine Heirat oder die Geburt eines
Babys ansteht. Bei einer Heirat lädt die Brautjungfer oder auch
eine nahe Verwandte Freundinnen und Nachbarinnen zu einer
gemütlichen Feier, einer wedding shower, zu sich nach Hause
ein. Von den Gästen wird erwartet, dass sie Geschenke mitbrin-
gen, die dann als Teil der Party von der Braut ausgepackt werden.
Eine baby shower wird meist von einer guten Freundin für die
werdende Mutter ausgerichtet. Die Gäste (wieder nur Frauen) bringen Geschenke für das Baby mit und werden natürlich bewirtet.

8 **Triangle**

mochte früher

had planted earlier in the spring. Pete used to like that smell. Now, though, it made him sick to his stomach.

Streifen

Mo inspected her nails for streaks and pretended to be bored with the idea of him going to see Doug, who was her boss, an 'important' guy who covered the whole East Coast territory. He'd invited both Mo and Pete to his country place but she'd planned a wedding shower for her niece. Doug had said to Pete, 'Well, why don't you come on down solo?' Pete had said he'd think about it.

zuständig war

für

Oh, sure she *seemed* bored with the idea of him going by himself. But she was a lousy actress; Pete could tell she was really excited at the thought and he knew why. But he just watched the lightning bugs and kept quiet. Played dumb. Unlike Mo, he *could* act.

Leuchtkäfer

nippten an

They were silent and sipped their drinks, the ice clunking dully in the plastic glasses. It was the first day of summer and there must've been a thousand lightning bugs in their front yard.

(= kind of) •

und zuckte ...

zusammen

'I know I kinda said I'd clean up the garage,' he said, wincing a little. 'But – '

'No, that can keep. I think it's a great idea, going down there.'

Übung 1 Setzen Sie die folgenden Sätze und Fragen in die indirekte Rede. Verwenden Sie dazu die eingeklammerten Wörter und achten Sie auf die passende Zeitform. Beispiel: Pete said: 'I will think about it.' wird zu: Pete said he would think about it.

1. Doug had said to Pete 'Well, why don't you come on down solo?'
Doug had suggested to Pete that he _____ (come) on down solo.
Doug had asked Pete why _____ (do not) he come on down solo.

I *know* you think it'd be a *great* idea, Pete thought. But he didn't say this to her. Lately he'd been thinking a lot of things and not saying them.

Pete was sweating – more from excitement than from the heat – and he wiped the moisture off his face and his short-cut blond hair with a napkin.

The phone rang and Mo went to answer it.

She came back and said, 'It's your *father*,' in that sour voice of hers. She sat down and didn't say anything else, just picked up her drink and examined her nails again.

Pete got up and went into the kitchen. His father lived in Wisconsin, not far from Lake Michigan. He loved the man and wished they lived closer together. Mo, though, didn't like him one bit and always raised a stink when Pete wanted to go visit. Pete was never exactly sure what the problem was between Mo and the man. But it made him mad that she treated him badly and would never talk to Pete about it.

machte ... Stunk

And he was mad too that Mo seemed to put Pete in the middle of things. Sometimes Pete even felt guilty he *had* a father.

He enjoyed talking but hung up after only five minutes

2. 'I know I said I'd clean up the garage,' he said.
He said he _____ (know) that he _____ (say) that he _____ (will clean up) the garage.

3. She said 'No, that can keep. I think it's a great idea.'
She said that no, it _____ (can) keep. She _____ (think) it _____ (be) a great idea.

4. I know you think it'd be a great idea, Pete thought.
Pete thought that he _____ (know) she _____ (think) it'd be a great idea.

5. She came back and said 'It's your father.'
She came back and said it _____ (be) his father.

10   Triangle

because he felt Mo didn't want him to be on the phone. Pete walked out onto the porch. 'Saturday. I'll go visit Doug then.'

Mo said, 'I think Saturday'd be fine.'

Fine …

They went inside and watched TV for a while. Then, at eleven Mo looked at her watch and stretched and said, 'It's getting late. Time for bed.'

And when Mo said it was time for bed, it was definitely time for bed.

Later that night, when she was asleep, Pete walked downstairs into the office. He reached behind a row of books resting on the built-in bookshelves and pulled out a large, sealed envelope.

Einbau- • zugeklebt

He carried it down to his workshop in the basement. He opened the envelope and took out a book.

It was called *Triangle* and Pete had found it in the true-crime section of a local used-book shop after flipping through nearly twenty books about real-life murders. Pete had never stolen anything in his life but that day he'd looked around the store and slipped the book

wahr

Übung 2   Im Englischen werden häufig zusammengezogene Verbformen verwendet, zum Beispiel „I'd like to go out." anstelle von „I would like to go out." Geben Sie bei den folgenden Sätzen die ausgeschriebene Verbform an.

1. Mo didn't want him to be on the phone.
2. I'll go visit Doug then.
3. I think Saturday'd be fine.
4. It's getting late.
5. He'd looked around the store.
6. He'd had to steal it.

inside his windbreaker then strolled casually out of the store. He'd *had* to steal it; he was afraid that – if everything went as he'd planned – the clerk might remember him buying the book and the police would use it as evidence.

Triangle was the true story of a couple in Colorado Springs. The wife was married to a man named Roy. But she was also seeing another man – Hank – a local carpenter and a friend of the family. Roy found out and waited until Hank was out hiking on a mountain path, then he snuck up and pushed him over a cliff. Hank grabbed on to a tree root but he lost his grip – or Roy smashed his hands; it wasn't clear – and Hank fell a hundred feet to his death on the rocks in the valley. Roy went back home and had a drink with his wife just to watch her reaction when the call came that Hank was dead.

Pete didn't know squat about crimes. All he knew was what he'd seen on TV and in the movies. None of the criminals in those shows seemed very smart and they were always getting caught by the good guys, even though *they* didn't really seem much smarter than the bad guys. But that crime in Colorado was a smart

Windjacke •

lässig •

Verkäufer

Beweis

Zimmermann

schlich ... sich heran • Halt

nichts

Ersetzen Sie die blau markierten Wörter durch ein Synonym, also ein Wort mit gleicher oder ähnlicher Bedeutung.

Übung 3

1. He strolled casually out of the store.
2. She was seeing another man.
3. He snuck up and pushed him over a cliff.
4. Pete didn't know squat about crimes.
5. Hank grabbed on to a tree root but he lost his grip.
6. None of the criminals in those shows seemed very smart.

12   Triangle

crime. Because there were no murder weapons and
very few clues. The only reason Roy got caught was
that he'd forgotten to look for witnesses.

*If the killer had only taken the time to look around
him, he would have seen the campers, who had a perfect view of Hank Gibson plummeting to his bloody
death, screaming as he fell, and of Roy standing on
the cliff, watching him…*

Triangle became Pete's bible. He read it cover to
cover – to see how Roy had planned the crime and to
find out how the police had investigated it.

Tonight, with Mo asleep, Pete read *Triangle* once
again. Paying particular attention to the parts he'd
underlined. Then he walked back upstairs, packed the
book in the bottom of his suitcase and lay on the couch
in the office, looking out the window at the hazy summer stars and thinking about his trip to Maryland from
every angle.

Because he wanted to make sure he got away with the
crime. He didn't want to go to jail for life – like Roy.

Oh, sure there were risks. Pete knew that. But nothing
was going to stop him.

Doug had to die.

Margin glosses:
Spuren

der … stürzte

von Anfang bis Ende

trüb

ungestraft davon- kam mit

Übung 4   Vervollständigen Sie die Bedingungssätze. Nicht vergessen: Im if-Satz steht kein ´would!

1. Roy got caught because he'd forgotten to look for witnesses.
   If Roy _____ to look for witnesses he _____ caught.
2. He read it cover to cover to see how Roy had planned the crime.
   If he _____ it cover to cover he _____
   how Roy had planned the crime.
3. He made sure he got away with the crime. Otherwise he would
   go to jail for life.
   If he _____ he got away with the crime he
   _____ to jail for life.

Pete realized he'd been thinking about the idea, in the back of his mind, for months, not long after Mo met Doug.

She worked for a drug company in Westchester – the same company Doug was a sales manager for, with his office in the company's headquarters in Baltimore. They met when he came to the branch office in New York for a sales conference. Mo had told Pete that she was having dinner with 'somebody' from the company but she didn't say who. Pete didn't think anything of it until he overheard her tell one of her girlfriends on the phone about this interesting guy she was working for. But then she realized Pete was standing near enough to hear and she changed the subject.

Over the next few months Pete noticed that Mo was getting distracted, paying less and less attention to him. And he heard her mention Doug more and more. One night Pete asked her about him.

'Oh, Doug?' she said, sounding irritated. 'Why, he's my boss. And a friend. That's all. Can't I have friends? Aren't I allowed?'

Pete noticed that Mo was starting to spend a lot of time on the phone and online. He tried to check the phone

Pharma-unternehmen

Zweigstelle

zufällig mitbekam

gereizt

Ersetzen Sie die blau markierten Wörter durch gleichbedeutende Wörter oder Wendungen aus dem Text.

Übung 5

1. Triangle became the code by which Pete lived.
2. He read the book from beginning to end.
3. He wanted to make sure he wasn't caught.
4. She talked about something else.
5. 'Oh Doug?' she said, sounding annoyed.
6. Mo was starting to spend a lot of time on the internet.

14 Triangle

bills to see if she was calling Baltimore but she hid
them or threw them out. He also tried to read her e-
mails but found she'd changed her pass-code. Pete's
specialty was computers, though, and he easily broke
into her account. But when he went to read her e-mails
he found she'd deleted them all on the main server.
He was so furious he nearly smashed the computer.

Bestürzung Then, to Pete's dismay, Mo started inviting Doug to
dinner at their house when he was in Westchester on

schlüpfrig- company business. He was older than Mo and sort of
schleimig • heavy. Slick–slimy, in Pete's opinion. Those dinners

sich bei ... were the worst ... They'd all three sit at the dinner
einzuschmei- table and Doug would try to charm Pete and ask him

cheln • about computers and sports and the things that Mo
dass Pete auf sie obviously had told Doug that Pete was into. But it was

stand • dass ... awkward and you could tell he didn't give a damn
ihm scheißegal about Pete. He kept glancing at Mo when he thought

war • Pete wasn't looking.

spionierte ... By then Pete was checking up on Mo all the time.
nach Sometimes he'd pretend to go to a game with some

friends but he'd come home early and find that she was
gone too. Then she'd get home at eight or nine and

durcheinander look all flustered, not expecting to find him, and she'd

---

Übung 6   Sind die folgenden Aussagen wahr oder falsch?
Tragen Sie ein T für true oder ein F für false in die Kästchen ein.

1.   Doug seemed genuinely interested in Pete.
2.   Mo had told Doug about Pete's interest in computers and
sports.
3.   Pete enjoyed having dinner with Mo and Doug.
4.   Pete found out about the relationship between Doug and
Mo through a letter in Mo's purse.
5.   Pete planned to kill Doug.
6.   Pete came up with a murder plan after watching a film.

Triangle   15

say she'd been working late even though she was just
an office manager and hardly ever worked later than   Büroleiterin
five before she met Doug. Once, when she claimed she
was at the office, Pete called Doug's number in Baltimore and the message said he'd be out of town for a
couple of days.

Everything was changing. Mo and Pete would have
dinner together but it wasn't the same as it used to be.
They didn't have picnics and they didn't take walks in
the evenings. And they hardly ever sat together on the
porch anymore and looked out at the fireflies and   Leuchtkäfer
made plans for trips they'd wanted to take.

'I don't like him,' Pete said. 'Doug, I mean.'

'Oh, quit being so jealous. He's a good friend, that's all.   hör auf
He likes both of us.'

'No, he doesn't like me.'

'Of course he does. You don't have to worry.'

But Pete did worry and he worried even more when he
found a Post-It note in her purse last month. It said,   Haftnotiz •
D.G.- Sunday, motel 2 p.m.   Handtasche

Doug's last name was Grant.

That Sunday morning Pete tried not to react when Mo
said, 'I'm going out for a while, honey.'

7.   Mo hoped that Pete and Doug would get along.

8.   Mo and Pete used to spend a lot of time together before
         Mo met Doug.

9.   Life had been very different for Pete before Mo had met
         Doug.

10. Mo changed a lot after she met Doug.

11. Mo and Pete planned to go on a trip together.

12. Mo was going to meet Doug on Sunday afternoon.

16 Triangle

'Where?'

'Shopping. I'll be back by five.'

He thought about asking her exactly where she was going but he didn't think that was a good idea. It might make her suspicious. So he said cheerfully, 'Okay, see you later.'

misstrauisch •
fröhlich •
Auffahrt

As soon as her car had pulled out of the driveway he'd started calling motels in the area and asking for Douglas Grant.

The clerk at the Westchester Motor Inn said, 'One minute, please. I'll connect you.'

Pete hung up fast.

ja

He was at the motel in fifteen minutes and, yep, there was Mo's car parked in front of one of the doors. Pete snuck up close to the room. The shade was drawn and the lights were out but the window was partly open. Pete could hear bits of the conversation.

Rollo • her-
untergezogen

'I don't like that.'

'That ...?' she asked.

'That color. I want you to paint your nails red. It's sexy. I don't like that color you're wearing. What is it?'

'Peach.'

'I like bright red,' Doug said.

Übung 7   Setzen Sie die Verben in die passende Zeitform. Orientieren Sie sich dabei am Rest des Satzes.

1. The clerk at the motel said that he _____ (connect) Pete.

2. Before someone had answered the telephone Pete _____ (hang up).

3. While Mo and Doug _____ (talk) inside the motel room Pete _____ (listen) outside to their conversation.

4. Doug told Mo he _____ (want) her to paint her nails bright red.

5. Recently Mo _____ (paint) her nails peach.

'Well, okay.'

There was some laughing. Then a long silence. Pete tried to look inside but he couldn't see anything. Finally, Mo said, 'We have to talk. About Pete.'

'He knows something,' Doug was saying. 'I know he does.'

'He's been like a damn spy lately,' she said, with that edge to her voice that Pete hated. 'Sometimes I'd like to strangle him.'

Schärfe

Pete closed his eyes when he heard Mo say this. Pressed the lids closed so hard he thought he might never open them again.

He heard the sound of a can opening.

Dose

Doug said, 'So what if he finds out?'

'So *what*? I told you what having an affair does to alimony in this state? It *eliminates* it. We have to be careful. I've got a lifestyle I'm accustomed to.'

Unterhaltszah-
lungen • an den
ich gewöhnt bin

'Then what should we do?' Doug asked.

'I've been thinking about it. I think you should do something with him.'

'Do something with him?' Doug had an edge to his voice too. 'Get him a one-way ticket …'

'Come on.'

Vervollständigen Sie die folgenden Sätze mit dem passenden Wort. (quiet, sarcastic, used, upset, worried)

Übung 8

1. Pete was _____ when he heard what Mo said.
2. Pete kept _____ while he listened to Mo and Doug talking.
3. Mo was _____ that Pete might find out about her affair.
4. Mo was _____ to a certain lifestyle.
5. Doug was being _____ when he was talking about doing something with Pete.

18   Triangle

'Okay, baby, sorry. But what do you mean by do some-thing?'

'Get to know him.'

Du machst
Scherze. •   'You're kidding.'

'Prove to him you're just my boss.'

beweise

Doug laughed and said in a soft, low voice, 'Does *that* feel like I'm just a boss?'

She laughed too. 'Stop it. I'm trying to have a serious talk here.'

'So, what? We go to a ball game together?'

'No, it's got to be more than that. Ask him to come visit you.'

arrogant

'Oh, that'd be fun.' With that same snotty tone that Mo sometimes used.

She continued, 'No, I like it. Ask us both to come down – maybe the weekend I'm having that shower for my niece. I won't be able to make it. Maybe he'll come by

macht die Stadt
unsicher

himself. You two hang out, paint the town. Pretend you've got a girlfriend or something.'

'He won't believe that.'

wenn es um ...
geht •

'Pete's only smart when it comes to computers and sports. He's stupid about everything else.'

verstauchte sich

Pete wrung his hands together. Nearly sprained a

Übung 9   Setzen Sie die folgenden unregelmäßigen Verben in die angegebene Zeitform.

1. Doug _____ to know Pete. (get – past tense)

2. It _____ like he was the boss. (feel – past perfect)

3. Pete and Doug _____ to a ball game together. (go – past tense)

4. They _____ him on the weekend. (see – past tense)

5. Doug and Pete _____ together. (hang out – past tense)

6. Pete was only smart when it _____ to computers and sports. (come – past tense)

7. Pete _____ his hands together. (wring – past perfect)

thumb – like the time he jammed his finger on the basketball court.

'That means I have to pretend I like him.'

'Yeah, that's *exactly* what it means. It's not going to kill you.'

'Pick another weekend. You come with him.'

'No,' she said. 'I'd have trouble keeping my hands off you.'

A pause. Then Doug said, 'Oh, hell, all right. I'll do it.'

Pete, crouching on a strip of yellow grass beside three discarded soda cans, shook with fury. It took all his willpower not to scream.

He hurried home, threw himself down on the couch in the office and turned on the game.

When Mo came home – which wasn't at five at all, like she promised, but at six-thirty – he pretended he'd fallen asleep.

That night he decided what he had to do. The next day he went to the book store and stole the copy of *Triangle*.

On Saturday Mo drove him to the airport.

'You two're gonna have fun together?'

sich ... einge-
klemmt hatte

so tun als ob

such ... aus

der ... kauerte •
weggeworfen •
Getränkedosen

werdet

8. Doug _____ his hands _____ Mo.
(keep off – past tense)

9. It _____ all his willpower not to scream.
(take – past perfect)

10. He _____ with fury. (shake – past tense)

11. He _____ himself down on the couch. (throw –
past perfect)

12. Mo _____ Pete to the airport. (drive – past perfect)

13. Pete _____ asleep. (fall – past tense)

14. He _____ to the bookstore. (go – past perfect)

15. He _____ a copy of 'Triangle'. (steal – past perfect)

Triangle

⌐ ob.

'You bet,' Pete said. He sounded cheerful because he *was* cheerful. 'We're gonna have a fine time.'

On the day of the murder, while his wife and her lover were sipping wine in a room at the Mountain View Lodge, Roy had lunch with a business associate. *The man, who wished to remain anonymous, reported that Roy was in unusually good* spirits. *It seemed his depression had* lifted *and he was happy once more.*

Fine, fine, fine …

Mo kissed him and then hugged him hard. He didn't kiss her back, though he did give her a hug, reminding himself that he had to be a good actor.

'You're looking forward to going, aren't you?' she asked.

'I sure am,' he answered. This was true.

'I love you,' she said.

'I love you too,' he responded.

This was not true. He hated her. He hoped the plane left on time. He didn't want to wait here with her any longer than he had to.

The flight attendant, a pretty blonde woman, kept stopping at his seat. This wasn't unusual for Pete.

Margin notes:
⌐ ob.
…chäftspart-ner •
Stimmung •
verflogen
umarmte
Stewardess

Übung 10 Adjektiv oder Adverb? Setzen Sie das eingeklammerte Wort in der richtigen Wortart in die Lücken ein. Beachten Sie: Manche Adjektive bekommen eine andere Bedeutung, wenn man -ly anhängt: hard = hart, aber hardly = kaum; short = kurz, aber shortly = bald; high = hoch, aber highly = sehr; near = nah, aber nearly = fast!

1. Roy was in an _____ good mood. (unusual)
2. Pete gave Mo a really _____ hug. (hard)
3. Mo thought that Pete _____ loved her. (genuine)
4. He could _____ see through Mo. (easy)
5. Pete was acting very _____ . (good)

Triangle   **21**

Women liked him. He'd heard a million times that he was cute, he was handsome, he was charming. Women were always leaning close and telling him that. Touching his arm, squeezing his shoulder.

süß

But today he answered her questions with a simple yes or no. And kept reading *Triangle.* Reading the passages he'd underlined. Memorizing them.
Learning about fingerprints, about interviewing witnesses, about footprints and trace evidence. There was a lot he didn't understand but he did figure out how smart the cops were and that he'd have to be very careful if he was going to kill Doug and get away with it.
'We're about to land,' the flight attendant said. 'Could you put your seat belt on, please?' She smiled at him.
He clicked the belt on and went back to his book.
Hank Gibson's body had fallen one hundred and twelve feet. He'd landed on his right side and of the more than two hundred bones in the human body, he'd broken seventy-seven of them. His ribs had pierced all his major internal organs and his skull was flattened on one side.

Er lernte sie auswendig. • Fingerabdrücke • Spuren • rechnete sich aus

durchbohrt • Schädel

6. He had noticed that women would often stand _____ to him. (close)
7. He made _____ he read all the important passages in the book. (sure)
8. He knew he had to plan very _____. (careful)
9. Pete was _____ thinking about killing Doug. (serious)
10. Hank had fallen _____ onto his right side. (straight)
11. He was _____ injured. (severe)

elcome to Baltimore, where the local time is twelve
wenty-five,' the flight attendant said. 'Please remain
in your seat with the seat belt fastened until the plane
has come to a complete stop and the pilot has turned
off the *Fasten Seat Belt* sign. Thank you.'

*The medical examiner estimated that Hank was trav-
eling 80 mph when he struck the ground and that
death was virtually instantaneous.*

Welcome to Baltimore …

Doug met him at the airport. Shook his hand.
'How you doing?' Doug asked.
'Okay.'

This was so weird. Spending the weekend with a man
that Mo knew so well and that Pete hardly knew at all.
Going hiking with somebody he hardly knew at all.
Going to kill somebody he hardly knew at all …
He walked along beside Doug.

'I need a beer and some crabs,' Doug said as they got
into his car. 'You hungry?'

'Sure am.'

They stopped at the waterfront and went into an old
dive. The place stunk. It smelled like the cleanser Mo

Übung 11 In der Umgangssprache kürzen Amerikaner, so wie Doug und Pete
hier, oft ab. Wie lauten die folgenden Sätze in der vollständigen
Form?

1. How you doing?
2. You hungry?
3. Sure am.
4. Think you can handle two real men?
5. You have a girlfriend?

Triangle **23**

used on the floor when Randolf, their Labrador retriever puppy, made a mess on the carpet.

Welpe • machte

Doug whistled at the waitress before they'd even sat down. 'Hey, honey, think you can handle two real men?' He gave her the sort of grin he'd seen Doug give Mo a couple of times. Pete looked away, a little embarrassed but plenty disgusted.

kommst klar mit

peinlich berührt • angewidert

When they started to eat, Doug calmed down, though that was probably the beers more than the food. Like Mo got after her third glass of Gallo* in the evenings. Pete wasn't saying much. Doug tried to be cheerful. He talked and talked but it was just garbage. Pete didn't pay any attention.

Wein von der Firma Gallo • Mist

'Maybe I'll give my girlfriend a call,' Doug said suddenly. 'See if she wants to join us.'

'You have a girlfriend? What's her name?'

'Uhm, Cathy,' he said.

The waitress's name tag said, *Hi, I'm Cathleen.*

Namensschild

'That'd be fun,' Pete said.

'She might be going out of town this weekend.' He avoided Pete's eyes. 'But I'll call her later.'

Pete's only smart when it comes to computers and sports. He's stupid about everything else …

Die Brüder Ernest und Julio Gallo, Söhne eines italienischen Einwanderers, gründeten 1933 im San Joaquin Valley in Kalifornien das heute weltgrößte Weingut in Familienbesitz, das auch zweitgrößter Weinproduzent der USA ist. Den Durchbruch schafften sie 1957 mit einem Weinverschnitt namens „Thunderbird" (Donnervogel) aus weißem Portwein und Zitronensaft. Lange stand Gallo für billige Weine, aber nach und nach kaufte das Unternehmen hochwertige Weingüter auf, und kalifornische Weine bekamen einen guten Ruf.

info

24   Triangle

Finally Doug looked at his watch and said, 'So what do you feel like doing now?'

Pete pretended to think for a minute and asked, 'Any-place we can go hiking around here?'

'Hiking?'

Wanderwege •   'Like any mountain trails?'

nein   Doug finished his beer, shook his head. 'Naw, nothing like that I know of.'

Pete felt rage again – his hands were shaking, the blood roaring in his ears – but he covered it up pretty well and tried to think. Now, what was he going to do? He'd counted on Doug agreeing to whatever he wanted. He'd counted on a nice high cliff.

rauschte • ver-
barg es

Hank was traveling 80 mph when he struck the ground…

But then Doug continued. 'But if you want to be out-side, one thing we could do maybe is go hunting.'

Jagen

'Hunting?'

hat Saison   'Nothing good's in season now,' Doug said. 'But there's always rabbits and squirrels.'

'Well –'

überlegte   'I've got a couple guns we can use.' Pete debated for only a moment and then said, 'Okay. Let's go hunting.'

Übung 12   Verbinden Sie die Sätze mit dem richtigen Bindewort. Als Hilfestellung ist es am Ende des Satzes auf Deutsch angegeben.

1. _____ Pete had pretended to think for a minute he suggested going hiking somewhere. (nachdem)

2. Pete suggested going hiking _____ he had read about the murder in 'Triangle'. (weil)

3. _____ Doug suggested going hunting instead. (jedoch)

Triangle   25

'You shoot much?' Doug asked him.

'Some.'

In fact, Pete was a good shot. His father had taught   Schütze
him how to load and clean guns and how to handle
them. ('Never point it at anything unless you're pre-   richte es … auf
pared to shoot it.')

But Pete didn't want Doug to know he knew anything
about guns so he let the man show him how to load
the little twenty-two and how to pull the slide to cock   spannen •
it and where the safety was.   Sicherung

I'm a *much* better actor than Mo.

They were in Doug's house, which was pretty nice. It
was in the woods and it was a big place, full of stone
walls and glass. The furniture wasn't like the cheap
things Mo and Pete had. It was mostly antiques.

Which depressed Pete even more, made him angrier,
because he knew that Mo liked money and she liked
people who had money even if they were idiots, like
Doug.

When Pete looked at Doug's beautiful house he knew
that if Mo ever saw it then she'd want Doug even more.
Then he wondered if she *had* seen it. Pete had gone to

4. _____ Pete had planned to kill Doug in a hiking
accident he agreed to go hunting. (obwohl)

5. Pete pretended that he didn't know anything about guns
_____ Doug would not suspect anything. (damit)

6. _____ Doug was loading the gun Pete was watching him. (während)

7. _____ Pete saw Doug's house he realized that Mo
would love the luxury of it. (sobald)

8. Doug didn't seem to distrust Pete _____ even invited him into his house. (und)

26 Triangle

Wisconsin a few months ago, to see his father and cousins. Maybe Mo had come down here to spend the night with Doug.

'So,' Doug said. 'Ready?'

'Where're we going?' Pete asked.

eingezäunt

'There's a good field about a mile from here. It's not posted. Anything we can hit we can take.'

'Sounds good to me,' Pete said.

They got into the car and Doug pulled onto the road.

'Better put that seat belt on,' Doug warned. 'I drive like a crazy man.'

Pete was looking around the big, empty field.

Keine Men-
schenseele.

Not a soul.

'What?' Doug asked, and Pete realized that the man was staring at him.

'I said it's pretty quiet.'

vermasselt
hatten

And deserted. No witnesses. Like the ones who screwed up Roy's plans in *Triangle*.

'Nobody knows about this place. I found it by my little

ganz alleine

old lonesome.'

Übung 13

Ergänzen Sie die Lücken mit einem der folgenden phrasal verbs, also mit einem Verb mit Präposition.

(decide on, hit off, look around, make up, mess up, see off, turn out, work out)

1. Mo had taken Pete to the airport. She wanted to _____ him _____.

2. Mo was hoping Pete and Doug would get on well. She hoped they would _____ it _____.

3. Roy should have made sure there were no people witnessing the murder. They had _____ his plan.

Triangle **27**

Doug said this real proud, as if he'd discovered a cure
for cancer. 'Lessee.' He lifted his rifle and squeezed off
a round.

Crack…

He missed a can sitting about thirty feet away.

'Little rusty,' he said. 'But, hey, aren't we having fun?'

'Sure are,' Pete answered.

Doug fired again, three times, and hit the can on the
last shot. It leapt into the air. 'There we go!'

Doug reloaded and they started through the tall grass
and brush.

They walked for five minutes.

'There,' Doug said. 'Can you hit that rock over there?'

He was pointing at a white rock about twenty feet
from them. Pete thought he could have hit it but he
missed on purpose. He emptied the clip.

'Not bad,' Doug said. 'Came close the last few shots.'

Pete knew he was being sarcastic.

Pete reloaded and they continued through the grass.

'So,' Doug said. 'How's she doing?'

'Fine. She's fine.'

Whenever Mo was upset and Pete'd ask her how she
was she'd say, 'Fine. I'm fine.'

(= Let's see.)
Mal sehen. •
drückte … ab

sprang • Na
bitte. •
Unterholz

zielte auf

Ladestreifen

4. If Roy had _____ he would have seen that there
were witnesses.

5. Doug thought that Pete was a beginner but it _____
that Pete was a good shot.

6. 'Triangle' was such a good story Pete didn't even have to
_____ a plan for himself.

7. When Pete realized that there was nowhere to go hiking he was
upset. He was afraid his plan wouldn't _____.

28 Triangle

Which didn't mean fine at all. It meant, I don't feel like telling you anything. I'm keeping secrets from you.

I don't love you anymore.

They stepped over a few fallen logs and started down a hill. The grass was mixed with blue flowers and daisies. Mo liked to garden and was always driving up to the nursery* to buy plants. Sometimes she'd come back without any and Pete began to wonder if, on those trips, she was really seeing Doug instead. He got angry again. Hands sweaty, teeth grinding together.

'She get her car fixed?' Doug asked. 'She was saying that there was something wrong with the transmission.'

How'd he know that? The car broke down only four days ago. Had Doug been there and Pete didn't know it?

Doug glanced at Pete and repeated the question.

Pete blinked. 'Oh, her car? Yeah, it's okay. She took it in and they fixed it.'

But then he felt better because that meant they *hadn't* talked yesterday or otherwise she would have told him about getting the car fixed.

Baumstämme •
Gänseblümchen

Gärtnerei

er knirschte mit
den Zähnen

Getriebe

---

info Das Wort nursery hat mehrere Bedeutungen. Hier im Text geht es um eine Gärtnerei, aber je nach dem Umfeld, in dem es steht, kann nursery auch Kindergarten oder Kinderzimmer heißen. Mit der Zusammensetzung nursery school ist eine Vorschule für Kinder zwischen drei und fünf Jahren gemeint, und ein nursery rhyme ist ein Reim oder Lied für kleine Kinder.

On the other hand, maybe Doug was lying to him now. Making it *look* as if she hadn't told him about the car when they really had talked.

Pete looked at Doug's pudgy face and couldn't decide whether to believe him or not. He looked sort of innocent but Pete had learned that people who seemed innocent were sometimes the most guilty. Roy, the husband in *Triangle*, had been a church choir director. From the smiling picture in the book, you'd never guess he'd kill somebody.

schwammig

Kirchenchor-leiter

Thinking about the book, thinking about murder.

Pete was scanning the field. Yes, there … About fifty feet away. A fence. Five feet high. It would work just fine.

suchte … mit den Augen ab •
Fuß (1 Fuß = 30,5 cm)

Fine…

As fine as Mo.

Who wanted Doug more than she wanted Pete.

'What're you looking for?' Doug asked.

'Something to shoot.'

And thought: Witnesses. That's what I'm looking for.

'Let's go that way,' Pete said and walked toward the fence.

Doug shrugged. 'Sure. Why not?'

zuckte mit den Schultern

Wie nursery gibt es viele englische Wörter, die mehr als eine Bedeutung haben. Finden Sie bei den folgenden Beispielen die zwei richtigen Bedeutungen und kreuzen Sie sie an.

Übung 14

1. lie	lügen	legen	liegen
2. scan	erkunden	scannen	absuchen
3. miss	verpassen	ausmisten	vermissen
4. bright	hell	herrlich	klug
5. sink	Waschbecken	untergehen	singen

30 Triangle

Pete studied it as they approached. Wood posts about eight feet apart, five strands of rusting wire.

Litzen • rostend • Stacheldraht

Not too easy to climb over but it wasn't barbed wire like some of the fences they'd passed. Besides, Pete didn't want it *too* easy to climb. He'd been thinking. He had a plan.

Roy had thought about the murder for weeks. It had obsessed his every waking moment. He'd drawn charts and diagrams and planned every detail down to the nth degree. In his mind, at least, it was the perfect crime.

bis ins kleinste Detail

Pete now asked, 'So what's your girlfriend do?'

'Uhm, my girlfriend? She works in Baltimore.'

'Oh. Doing what?'

'In an office. Big company.'

'Oh.'

They got closer to the fence. Pete asked, 'You're divorced? Mo was saying you're divorced.'

haben uns ... getrennt

'Right. Betty and I split up two years ago.'

'You still see her?'

'Who? Betty? Naw. We went our separate ways.'

'You have any kids?'

nein

'Nope.'

Übung 15 Im folgenden Text sind fünf sachliche Fehler versteckt. Können Sie sie finden?

Pete was spying on Mo and Doug who were sitting in a restaurant. He couldn't see them but he listened to what they were saying. They were talking about moving in together. Mo was concerned about Pete knowing about their relationship because she didn't want him to divorce her. She was accustomed to having a certain amount of money and didn't want to give up her lifestyle. Pete nearly fainted when he heard that. Inside Doug was giggling and talked in a strange tone of voice about dealing with Pete.

Of course not. When you had kids you had to think about somebody else. You couldn't think about yourself all the time.

Like Doug did.

Like Mo.

Pete was looking around again. For squirrels, for rabbits, for witnesses.

Then Doug stopped and he looked around too. Pete wondered why but then Doug took a bottle of beer from his knapsack and drank the whole bottle down and tossed it on the ground. 'You want something to drink?' Doug asked.

Rucksack •
warf

'No,' Pete answered. It was good that Doug'd be slightly drunk when they found him. They'd check his blood. They did that. That's how they knew Hank'd been drinking when they got what was left of the body (80 mph, after all) to the Colorado Springs hospital – they checked the alcohol in the blood.

untersuchen

The fence was only twenty feet away.

'Oh, hey,' Pete said. 'Over there. Look.'

He pointed to the grass on the other side of the fence.

'What?' Doug asked.

'I saw a couple of rabbits.'

Setzen Sie die fehlenden Reflexivpronomen in die Lücken ein. Beispiel: When you had kids you couldn't think about yourself all the time.

Übung 16

1. In Pete's opinion Mo and Doug only thought about _____.

2. Doug drank a whole bottle of beer by _____.

3. Mo was at home all by _____.

4. Pete thought that if Doug was gone Mo and he would be able to go hiking all by _____.

5. Doug said to Pete: 'Help _____ to a bottle of beer.'

32   Triangle

'You did? Where?'

'I'll show you. Come on.'

'Okay. Let's do it,' Doug said.

They walked to the fence. Suddenly Doug reached out and took Pete's rifle. 'I'll hold it while you climb over. Safer that way.'

erstarrte   Jesus … Pete *froze* with terror. He realized now that Doug was going to do exactly what Pete had in mind. He'd been planning on holding Doug's gun for him. And then when Doug was at the top of the fence he was going to shoot him. Making it look like Doug had tried to carry his gun as he climbed the fence but he'd dropped it and it went off.

Gesetzesregel   *Roy bet on the old* law enforcement rule *that what looks like an accident probably is an accident.*

Pete didn't move. He thought he saw something odd in Doug's eyes, something mean and sarcastic. It reminded him of Mo's expression. Pete took one look at those eyes and he could see how much Doug hated him and how much he loved Mo.

'You want me to go first?' Pete asked. Not moving, wondering if he should just run.

'Sure,' Doug said. 'You go first. Then I'll hand the guns

Übung 17   Ergänzen Sie die folgenden Sätze oder Fragen mit Frageanhängseln (question tags). So meint Pete in Dougs Augen zu lesen: 'You're not afraid of climbing over the fence, are you?'

1. Doug reached out and took Pete's rifle, _____?

2. Pete had been planning on holding Doug's gun for him, _____?

3. When Doug was at the top of the fence he was going to shoot him, _____?

over to you.' His eyes said, You're not afraid of climbing over the fence, are you? You're not afraid to turn your back on me, are you?

mir den Rücken zuzudrehen

Then Doug was looking around too.

Looking for witnesses, just like Pete had been.

'Go on,' Doug encouraged.

Pete – his hands shaking now from fear – started to climb. Thinking: This is it. He's going to shoot me. Last month I left the motel too early! Doug and Mo had kept talking and planned out how he was going to ask me down here and pretend to be all nice then he'd shoot me.

Remembering it was Doug who'd suggested hunting.

But if I run, Pete thought, he'll chase me down and shoot me. Even if he shoots me in the back he'll just claim it's an accident.

wird ... mich aufspüren

Roy's lawyer argued to the jury that, yes, the men had met on the path and struggled, but that Hank had fallen accidentally. He urged the jury to find that, at worst, Roy was guilty of negligent homicide.

fahrlässiger Totschlag • Sprosse

He put his foot on the first rung of wire. Started up. Second rung of wire …

Pete's heart was beating a million times a minute. He

4. You want me to go first, _____?

5. Then I'll hand the guns over to you, _____?

6. Go on, _____?

7. This is it, _____ ?

8. He's going to shoot me, _____?

9. Last month I left the motel too early, _____?

10. If I run, he'll chase me down and shoot me, _____?

11. Even if he shoots me in the back he'll just claim it's an accident, _____?

34 Triangle

abzuwischen •	had to pause to wipe his palms.
Handflächen	He thought he heard a whisper, as if Doug were talking to himself.

He swung his leg over the top wire.

Then he heard the sound of a gun cocking.

And Doug said in a hoarse whisper, 'You're dead.'

schnappte nach   Pete gasped.

Luft •   *Crack!*

zackig   The short, snappy sound of the twenty-two filled the field.

unterdrückte   Pete choked a cry and looked around, nearly falling off the fence.

'Damn,' Doug muttered. He was aiming away from the

Baumgrenze •   fence. Nodding toward a tree line. 'Squirrel. Missed

Inches (1 Inch =   him by two inches.'

2,54 cm)   'Squirrel,' Pete repeated manically. 'And you missed him.'

'Two goddamn inches.'

Hands shaking, Pete continued over the fence and climbed to the ground.

'You okay?' Doug asked. 'You look a little funny.'

'I'm fine,' he said.

Fine, fine, fine…

Übung 18   Wen beschreiben die folgenden Sätze – Roy, Doug, Mo oder Pete?
Setzen Sie die richtigen Namen und die fehlenden Pronomen ein.

1. _____ didn't trust _____.
2. _____ probably hadn't imagined _____ would spend _____ life in prison.
3. _____ tried to shoot a squirrel.
4. _____ was first to climb the fence even though he didn't really want to.
5. _____ suggested shooting a rabbit.

Triangle **35**

Doug handed Pete the guns and started over the fence. Pete debated. Then he put his rifle on the ground and gripped Doug's gun tight. He walked to the fence so that he was right below Doug.

'Look,' Doug said as he got to the top. He was strad-dling it, his right leg on one side of the fence, his left on the other. 'Over there.' He pointed nearby.

saß rittlings darauf

There was a big gray lop-eared rabbit on his haunches only twenty feet away.

mit Hängeohren
• Hinterläufen

'There you go!' Doug whispered. 'You've got a great shot.'

Pete shouldered the gun. It was pointing at the ground, halfway between the rabbit and Doug.

'Go ahead. What're you waiting for?'

Roy was convicted of premeditated murder in the first degree and sentenced to life in prison. Yet he came very close to committing the perfect murder. If not for a simple twist of fate he would have gotten away with it.

vorsätzlich •
Mord •
verurteilt •
Wendung

Pete looked at the rabbit, looked at Doug.

'Aren't you going to shoot?'

Uhm, okay, he thought.

Pete raised the gun and pulled the trigger once.

6. _____ was probably thinking _____ and _____ were having a good time.

7. _____'s plan had been very close to perfect.

8. _____ tried to find a chance to shoot _____.

9. _____ was very nervous as he thought _____ might shoot him any minute.

10. _____ had suggested going hunting.

Doug gasped, pressed at the tiny bullethole in his chest. 'But ... But ... No!'

He fell backwards off the fence and lay on a patch of dried mud, completely still. The rabbit bounded through the grass, panicked by the sound of the shot, and disappeared in a tangle of bushes that Pete recognized as blackberries. Mo had planted tons of them in their backyard.

hoppelte

Brombeeren •
sie massenweise

The plane descended from cruising altitude and slowly floated toward the airport.

Pete watched the billowy clouds and his fellow passengers, read the in-flight magazine and the (Sky Mall) catalog.

Reiseflughöhe

schwadenartig •
Bordmagazin

He was bored. He didn't have his book to read. Before he'd talked to the Maryland state troopers* about Doug's death he'd thrown *Triangle* into a trash bin.

One of the reasons the jury convicted Roy was that, upon examining his house, the police found several books about disposing of evidence. Roy had no satisfactory explanation for them.

The small plane glided out of the skies and landed at

Staatspolizisten

• Mülleimer

Beseitigung von
Beweismaterial

info

Jeder amerikanische Bundesstaat hat eine eigene Staatspolizei. In Maryland wurde die Staatspolizei 1935 vom Gouverneur von Maryland gegründet. Damals arbeiteten die state troopers zu Pferd und auf Motorrädern. In der militärähnlichen Struktur der Polizei stehen die Trooper auf der untersten Stufe, sind also einfache Polizisten, die für Unfallberichte, Einbrüche und Familienzwistigkeiten zuständig sind. Nach drei Jahren können sie allerdings zu Troopern erster Klasse befördert werden.

White Plains airport. Pete pulled his knapsack out from underneath the seat in front of him and climbed out of the plane. He walked down the ramp, beside the flight attendant, a tall black woman, talking with her about the flight.

Pete saw Mo at the gate. She looked numb. She wore sunglasses and Pete supposed she'd been crying. She was clutching a Kleenex in her fingers.

wie betäubt

hielt ... um-klammert

Her nails weren't bright red anymore, he noticed.

They weren't peach either.

They were just plain fingernail color.

The flight attendant came up to Mo. 'You're Mrs. Jill Anderson?'

Mo nodded.

The woman held up a sheet of paper. 'Here. Could you sign this please?'

Numbly, Mo took the pen the woman offered and signed the paper.

It was an unaccompanied-minor form, which adults had to sign to allow their children to get on planes by themselves. The parent picking up the child also had to sign it. After his parents were divorced Pete flew back and forth between his dad in Wisconsin and his

Formular für alleinreisende Kinder

Setzen Sie die passenden Bindewörter in die Lücken ein.
(either ... or, neither ... nor, both ... and)

Übung 19

1. Pete had gotten rid of _____ 'Triangle' _____ Doug.
2. Mo's fingernails were painted _____ bright red _____ peach.
3. _____ Mo was going to believe Pete was innocent _____ not.
4. _____ Pete's father _____ his mother shared custody of him.
5. _____ the flight attendant _____ Mo suspected Pete of knowing anything.

38 Triangle

mother, Mo, in White Plains so often he knew all about airlines' procedures for kids who flew alone.

'I have to say,' she said to Mo, smiling down at Pete, 'he's the best behaved youngster I've ever had on one of my flights. How old are you, Pete?'

Kind

'I'm ten,' he answered. 'But I'm going to be eleven next week.'

She squeezed his shoulder. Then looked at Mo. 'I'm so sorry about what happened,' she said in a soft voice. 'The trooper who put Pete on the plane told me your boyfriend was killed in a hunting accident?'

'No,' Mo said, struggling to say the words, 'he wasn't my boyfriend.'

Though Pete was thinking: Of course he was your boyfriend. Except you didn't want the court to find that out because then Dad wouldn't have to pay you alimony anymore. Which is why she and Doug had been working so hard to convince Pete that Doug was 'just a friend.'

Can't I have friends? Aren't I allowed?

No, you're not, Pete thought. You're not going to get

fallen zu lassen

away with dumping your son the way you dumped Dad.

Übung 20

Sind die folgenden Aussagen wahr oder falsch?
Tragen Sie ein T für true oder ein F für false in die Kästchen ein.

1. The twist of the story is that Pete turns out to be Mo's brother.
2. Pete has succeeded in committing the 'perfect' murder.
3. Pete had planned Doug's murder to punish Mo for dumping his father.
4. The flight attendant and everybody else including Mo seem to feel sorry for Pete.

Triangle   **39**

'Can we go home, Mo?' he asked, looking as sad as he
could. 'I feel real funny about what happened.'

komisch

'Sure, honey.'

'Mo?' the flight attendant asked.

Mo, staring out the window, said, 'My name's Jill. But
when he was five Pete tried to write *mother* on my
birthday card. He just wrote *M-O* and didn't know how
to spell the rest. It became my nickname.'

'What a sweet story,' the woman said and looked like
she was going to cry. 'Pete, you come back and fly with
us real soon.'

'Okay.'

'Hey, what're you going to do for your birthday?'

'I don't know,' he said. Then he looked up at his mother. 'I was thinking about maybe going hiking. In Colorado. Just the two of us.'

5. Mo is devastated but still won't admit that Doug was her
boyfriend.

6. Unfortunately Pete had forgotten to throw away 'Triangle'.

7. Doug would have liked to get rid of Pete to have Mo to
himself.

8. Pete's father lived in Colorado.

9. Doug was leaving behind a wife and two daughters.

10. Pete is not even eleven years old.

For Services Rendered

geleistete Dienste

'At first I thought it was me … but now I know for sure: My husband's trying to drive me crazy.'

Dr. Harry Bernstein nodded and, after a moment's pause, dutifully noted his patient's words on the steno pad resting on his lap.

pflichtbewusst

'I don't mean he's *irritating* me, driving me crazy that way – I mean he's making me question my sanity. And he's doing it on purpose.'

infrage stellen

Patsy Randolph, facing away from Harry on his leather couch, turned to look at her psychiatrist. Even though he kept his Park Avenue office quite dark during his sessions he could see that there were tears in her eyes.

Sitzungen

'You're very upset,' he said in a kind tone.

'Sure, I'm upset,' she said. 'And I'm scared.'

habe Angst

This woman, in her late forties, had been his patient for two months. She'd been close to tears several times

---

Vervollständigen Sie die folgenden Sätze mit dem passenden Wort. (insanity, afraid, intended, patient, troubled)

Übung 21

1. Patsy Randolph was Dr. Harry Bernstein's _____.

2. Patsy claimed her husband was driving her to _____.

3. She was _____ of her husband.

4. Harry could see Patsy was _____.

5. She believed her husband _____ to drive her crazy.

42 For Services Rendered

during their sessions but had never actually cried. Tears are important barometers of emotional weather. Some patients go for years without crying in front of their doctors and when the eyes begin to water any competent therapist sits up and takes notice.

Oberschenkel

Harry studied Patsy closely as she turned away again and picked at a button on the cushion beside her thigh. 'Go on,' he encouraged. 'Tell me about it.'

zupfte … heraus

• betupfte •

makellos

She snagged a Kleenex from the box beside the couch. Dabbed at her eyes but she did so carefully; as always, she wore impeccable makeup.

'Please,' Harry said in a soft voice.

widerwillig

'It's happened a couple of times now,' she began reluctantly. 'Last night was the worst. I was lying in bed and I heard this voice. I couldn't really hear it clearly at first. Then it said …' She hesitated. 'It said it was my father's ghost.'

Motifs in therapy didn't get any better than this, and Harry paid close attention.

'You weren't dreaming?'

auf und ab zu

gehen •

war verzweifelt

'No, I was awake. I couldn't sleep and I'd gotten up for a glass of water. Then I started walking around the apartment. Just pacing. I felt frantic. I lay back in bed.

Übung 22 Ersetzen Sie die blau markierten Wörter durch gleichbedeutende Wörter oder Wendungen aus dem Text.

1. Tears are important signs of emotional weather.
2. Harry looked at Patsy closely.
3. Patsy wore perfect makeup.
4. Patsy told him that it had happened several times.
5. Harry listened closely to what Patsy said.
6. Patsy was walking back and forth across the room.
7. She told Harry that the ghost just talked forever and ever.

For Services Rendered **43**

And the voice – I mean, *Pete's* voice – said that it was my father's ghost.'

'What did he say?'

'He just rambled on and on. Telling me about all kinds of things from my past. Incidents from when I was a girl. I'm not sure. It was hard to hear.'

quasselte … ohne Ende

'And these were things your husband knew?'

'Not all of them.' Her voice cracked. 'But he could've found them out. Looking through my letters and my yearbooks. Things like that.'

versagte

'You're sure he was the one talking?'

'The voice sounded sort of like Peter's. Anyway, who else would it be?' She laughed, her voice nearly a cackle. 'I mean, it could hardly be my father's ghost, now, could it?'

Gackern

'Maybe he was just talking in his sleep.'

She didn't respond for a minute. 'See, that's the thing … He wasn't in bed. He was in the den, playing some video game.'

Arbeitszimmer

Harry continued to take his notes.

'And you heard him from the den?'

'He must have been at the door … Oh, doctor, it sounds ridiculous. I know it does. But I think he was

8. It was difficult to understand what the ghost was saying.

9. The ghost was talking about events from her childhood.

10. The voice sounded a bit like her husband's voice.

11. Patsy didn't reply for a minute.

12. Harry kept writing down his observations.

13. Patsy admitted it sounded silly.

kneeling at the door – it's right next to the bedroom – and was whispering.'

'Did you go into the den? Ask him about it?'

'I walked to the door real fast but by the time I opened it he was back at the desk.' She looked at her hands and found she'd shredded the Kleenex. She glanced at Harry to see if he'd noticed the compulsive behavior, which of course he had, and then stuffed the tissue into the pocket of her expensive beige slacks.

zerrupft •
zwanghaft

Hosen

'And then?'

'I asked him if he'd heard anything, any voices. And he looked at me like I was nuts and went back to his game.'

verrückt wäre

'And that night you didn't hear any more voices?'

'No.'

Harry studied his patient. She'd been a pretty girl in her youth, he supposed, because she was a pretty woman now (therapists *always* saw the child within the adult). Her face was sleek and she had the slightly upturned nose of a Connecticut socialite* who debates long and hard about having rhinoplasty but never does. He recalled that Patsy'd told him her weight was never a problem: she'd hire a personal

gepflegt •
Stupsnase •
eine Nasen-
korrektur

---

info Socialites werden meist weibliche Mitglieder der amerikanischen feinen Gesellschaft oder der Aristokratie genannt, die vor allem damit beschäftigt sind, Bälle und Partys zu besuchen und dabei gesehen zu werden oder gesellschaftliche Anlässe zu organisieren. Heutzutage gehören nicht nur der Geldadel, sondern auch Neureiche dazu, die ihren Reichtum durch Geldanlagen erworben haben oder Teil des sogenannten Jetset sind. Es gibt sogar ein soziales Register, in dem die Angehörigen der sozialen Elite aufgeführt werden.

For Services Rendered 45

trainer whenever she gained five pounds. She'd said –
with irritation masking secret pride – that men often
tried to pick her up in bars and coffee shops.

sie abzuschleppen

He asked, 'You say this's happened before? Hearing the
voice?'

Another hesitation. 'Maybe two or three times. All
within the past couple of weeks.'

'But why would Peter want to drive you crazy?'

Patsy, who'd come to Harry presenting with the classic
symptoms of a routine midlife crisis, hadn't discussed
her husband much yet. Harry knew he was good-looking, a few years younger than Patsy, not particularly
ambitious. They'd been married for three years – second marriages for both of them – and they didn't seem
to have many interests in common. But of course that
was just Patsy's version. The 'facts' that are revealed in
a therapist's office can be very fishy. Harry Bernstein

zweifelhaft

worked hard to become a human lie detector and his
impression of the marriage was that there was much
unspoken conflict between husband and wife.

Patsy considered his question. 'I don't know. I was talking to Sally…' Harry remembered her mentioning
Sally, her best friend. She was another Upper East Side

Wen beschreiben die Adjektive – Harry, Patsy oder Peter?
Ordnen Sie den Wörtern den jeweils passenden Namen zu.

Übung 23

1. proud
2. good-looking
3. professional
4. upset
5. compulsive
6. concerned

46 For Services Rendered

Matrone	matron – one of the ladies who lunch – and was married to the president of one of the biggest banks in New York. 'She said that maybe Peter's jealous of me. I mean, look at us – I'm the one with the social life, I have the friends, I have the money...' He noticed a manic edge to her voice. She did too and controlled it. 'I just don't know why he's doing it. But he is.' 'Have you talked to him about this?'
streitet ... ab • bildeten sich	'I tried. But naturally he denies everything.' She shook her head and tears swelled in her eyes again. 'And then ... the birds.' 'Birds?' Another Kleenex was snagged, used and shredded. She didn't hide the evidence this time. 'I have this collection of ceramic birds. Made by Boehm. Do you know about the company?' 'No.' 'They're very expensive. They're German. Beautifully made. They were my parents.' When our father died Steve and I split the inheritance but he got most of the
Erbstücke	personal family heirlooms. That really hurt me. But I did get the birds.' Harry knew that her mother had died ten years ago

Übung 24   Setzen Sie die folgenden Sätze und Fragen in die indirekte Rede. Stellen Sie dabei jeweils „Patsy said/told Harry that ..." oder „Harry asked her whether/if ..." vor den Satz. Denken Sie daran, dass auch die Pronomen angepasst werden müssen.

1. Patsy: 'Sally said that maybe Peter's jealous of me.'
2. Patsy: 'I just don't know why Peter is doing it.'
3. Harry: 'Have you talked to him about this?'
4. Patsy: 'The ceramic birds are made by Boehm. Do you know about the company?'

For Services Rendered **47**

and her father about three years ago. The man had been very stern and had favored Patsy's older brother, Stephen. He had been patronizing to her all her life.

'I have four of them. There used to be five but when I was twelve I broke one. I ran inside – I was very excited about something and I wanted to tell my father about it – and I bumped into the table and knocked one off. The sparrow. It broke. My father spanked me with a willow switch and sent me to bed without dinner.'

Ah, an Important Event. Harry made a note but decided not to pursue the incident any further at that moment.

'And?'

'The morning after I heard my father's ghost for the first time …' Her voice grew harsh. 'I mean, the morning after *Peter* started whispering to me … I found one of the birds broken. It was lying on the living room floor. I asked Peter why he'd done it – he knows how important they were to me – and he denied it. He said I must have been sleepwalking and did it myself. But I know I didn't. Peter had to've been the one.' She'd slipped into her raw, irrational voice again.

Harry glanced at the clock. He hated the legacy of the

streng • bevorzugt • hatte sie … von oben herab behandelt

Spatz • versohlte mich • Weidenrute

scharf

verfiel in •

Erbe

---

5. Patsy: 'When our father died Steve and I split the inheritance but he got most of the family heirlooms.'

6. Patsy: 'When I was twelve I broke one of the birds. I ran inside – I was very excited about something and I wanted to tell my father about it.'

7. Harry: 'What happened yesterday?'

8. Patsy: 'The morning after Peter started whispering to me I found one of the birds broken.'

9. Harry: 'What exactly did you hear?'

48 For Services Rendered

psychoanalyst: the perfectly timed fifty-minute hour.

vertiefen There was so much more he wanted to delve into. But patients need consistency and, according to the old school, discipline. He said, 'I'm sorry but I see our time's up.'

unordentlich Dutifully Patsy rose. Harry observed how disheveled she looked. Yes, her makeup had been carefully applied but the buttons on her blouse weren't done properly. Either she'd dressed in a hurry or hadn't paid atten-

hellbraun tion. One of the straps on her expensive, tan shoes wasn't hooked.

She rose. 'Thank you, Doctor … It's good just to be able to tell someone about this.'

'We'll get everything worked out. I'll see you next week.'

After Patsy had left the office Harry Bernstein sat down

drehte sich at his desk. He spun slowly in his chair, gazing at his books – the *DSM-IV, The Psychopathology of Everyday Life*, the APA *Handbook of Neuroses*, volumes by Freud, Adler, Jung, Karen Horney, hundreds of others. Then looking out the window again, watching the late-

die … rasten afternoon sunlight fall on the cars and taxis speeding north on Park Avenue.

Übung 25 Jeweils eine der drei Aussagen ist wahr. Tragen Sie ein T für true oder ein F für false in die Kästchen ein.

1. Harry's sessions with his patients always lasted longer than planned.

Harry made sure his sessions never lasted longer than they were supposed to.

Harry timed his sessions according to his patient's needs.

For Services Rendered **49**

A bird flew past.

He thought about the shattered ceramic sparrow from Patsy's childhood.

And Harry thought: What a significant session this had been.

Not only for his patient. But for him too.

Patsy Randolph – who had until today been just another *mildly discontented* middle-aged patient – represented a *watershed event* for Doctor Harold David Bernstein. He was in a position to change her life completely.

leicht • unzufrieden • Wendepunkt

And in doing so maybe he could *redeem* his own.

retten

Harry laughed out loud, spun again in the chair, like a child on a playground. Once, twice, three times.

A figure appeared in the doorway. 'Doctor?' Miriam, his secretary, *cocked her head*, which was covered with *fuzzy* white hair. 'Are you all right?'

legte ihren Kopf auf die Seite • kraus

'I'm fine. Why're you asking?'

'Well, it's just … I don't think I've heard you laugh for a long time. I don't think I've *ever* heard you laugh in your office.'

Which was another reason to laugh. And he did.

runzelte die Stirn

She *frowned*, concern in her eyes.

2. Patsy always had a perfect appearance.
Patsy's makeup was smeared and her clothes were in a mess.
Apart from her makeup Patsy looked very untidy.

3. Harry felt unable to help Patsy.
Harry was frustrated about today's session.
Harry believed that today's session had been a crucial one.

4. Miriam was annoyed at her boss behaving like a child.
Miriam was used to Harry laughing out loud.
Miriam was surprised by Harry's behavior.

50 **For Services Rendered**

Harry stopped smiling. He looked at her gravely. 'Listen, I want you to take the rest of the day off.'

She looked mystified. 'But … it's quitting time, Doctor.'

'Joke,' he explained. 'It was a joke. See you tomorrow.'

Miriam eyed him cautiously, unable, it seemed to shake the quizzical expression from her face. 'You're sure you're all right?'

'I'm fine. Good night.'

'Night, Doctor.'

A moment later he heard the front door to the office click shut.

He spun around in his chair once more, reflecting: Patsy Randolph … I can save you and you can save me. And Dr. Harry Bernstein was a man badly in need of saving. Because he hated what he did for a living.

Not the business of helping patients with their mental and emotional problems – oh, he was a natural-born therapist. None better. What he hated was practicing Upper East Side* psychiatry. It had been the last thing he'd ever wanted to do. But in his second year of Columbia Medical School the tall, handsome student

Margin notes (left column):
- ernst
- verblüfft •
- Feierabend
- fragend
- der geborene

---

info

Die Upper East Side ist ein Stadtviertel in Manhattan, das den Ruf hat, das reichste und vornehmste Viertel ganz New Yorks zu sein. Bei Wahlen wird dort das meiste Geld in den ganzen USA für die Kandidaten gesammelt. Durch die Upper East Side führen die Madison Avenue, eine der teuersten Einkaufsmeilen der Welt, und die Fifth Avenue, die Museumsmeile genannt wird; dort steht unter anderem das berühmte Guggenheim Museum. Die Gegend ist Schauplatz vieler Kino- und Fernsehfilme, wie zum Beispiel „Frühstück bei Tiffany" und „Sex and the City".

For Services Rendered 51

met the tall, beautiful assistant development director of the Museum of Modern Art. Harry and Linda were married before he started his internship. He moved out of his fifth-floor walk-up near Harlem and into her townhouse on East Eighty-first. Within weeks she'd begun changing his life. Linda was a woman who had high aspirations for her man (very similar to Patsy, in whose offhand comment several weeks ago about her husband's lack of ambition Harry had seen reams of anger). Linda wanted money, she wanted to be on the regulars list for benefits at the Met, she wanted to be pampered at four-star restaurants in Eze and Monaco and Paris.

A studious, easygoing man from a modest suburb of New York, Harry knew that by listening to Linda he was headed in the wrong direction. But he was in love with her so he continued to listen. They bought a coop in a high-rise on Madison Avenue and he hung up his shingle (well, a heavy, brass plaque) outside this three-thousand-dollar-a-month office on Park and Seventy-eighth.

At first Harry had worried about the astronomical bills they were amassing. But soon the money was flowing

praktisches Jahr • Wohnung ohne Aufzug • Reihenhaus

beiläufig geäußert • tief

Gästeliste • Benefizveranstaltungen • verwöhnt

ging er • Apartment • Hochhaus • Schild • Messing

die sie anhäuften

Setzen Sie die eingeklammerten Verben in die Verlaufsform.   **Übung 26**

1. _____ (marry) seemed to be the right thing to do for Harry and Linda.
2. After the wedding he would be _____ (start) his internship.
3. Linda was quickly _____ (begin) to change Harry's life.
4. Harry's life was _____ (head) in the wrong direction.
5. He was _____ (hang up) his sign outside his office.
6. Harry was always _____ (worry) about the high bills.

For Services Rendered

in. He had no trouble getting business; there's no lack of neuroses among the rich, and the insured, on the isle of Manhattan. He was also very good at what he did. His patients came and they liked him and so they returned weekly.

'Nobody understands me, sure we've got money but money isn't everything and the other day my house-keeper looks at me like I'm from outer space and it's not my fault and I get so angry when my mother wants to go shopping on my one day off and I think Samuel's seeing someone and I think my son's gay and I just cannot lose these fifteen pounds ...'

Their troubles may have been plebeian, even laughably minor at times, but his oath, as well as his character, wouldn't let Harry minimize them. He worked hard to help his patients.

And all the while he neglected what he really wanted to do. Which was to treat severe mental cases. People who were paranoid schizophrenics, people with bipolar depression and borderline personalities – people who led sorrowful lives and couldn't hide from that sorrow with the money that Harry's patients had.

From time to time he had volunteered at various clin-

Margin notes:
Mangel an
plebejisch
Menschen mit schweren seeli-schen Störungen
• im Grenz-bereich •
ehrenamtlich geholfen

Übung 27 Formulieren Sie die folgenden Sätze um, sodass sie das Gegenteil aussagen.

1. Harry was very good at what he did.
2. His patients liked him and so they returned weekly.
3. Nobody understands me, sure we've got money but money isn't everything.
4. Their troubles were laughably minor at times.
5. He neglected what he really wanted to do.

For Services Rendered 53

ics – particularly a small one in Brooklyn that treated homeless men and women – but with his Park Avenue caseload and his wife's regimen of social obligations, there had been no way he could devote much time to the clinic. He'd wrestled with the thought of just chucking his Park Avenue practice. Of course, if he'd done that, his income would have dropped by ninety percent. He and Linda had had two children a couple of years after they'd gotten married – two sweet daughters Harry loved very much – and their needs, very *expensive* needs, private school sorts of needs, had taken priority over his personal contentment. Besides, as idealistic as he was in many ways, Harry had known that Linda would leave him in a flash if he'd started working full-time in Brooklyn.

But the irony was that even after Linda *did* leave him – for someone she'd met at one of the society benefits that Harry couldn't bear to attend – he hadn't been able to spend any more time at the clinic than he had when he'd been married. The debts Linda had run up while they were married were excruciating. His oldest daughter was in an expensive college and his younger was on her way to Vassar* next year.

Fällen • dem strengen Regiment • gerungen mit • hinzuschmeißen

auf der Stelle

die Schulden, die Linda gemacht hatte • unvorstellbar hoch

Vassar College gilt als eine der besten Elitehochschulen für Geisteswissenschaften. Es bietet rund 2400 Studienplätze, rangiert auf der gleichen Stufe wie Harvard und Princeton und liegt zwei Autostunden von New York City entfernt. 1861 wurde es als privates Frauencollege gegründet. Erst 1969 wurden offiziell auch männliche Studenten zugelassen. Die in den USA besonders an privaten Universitäten sehr hohen Studiengebühren betragen in Vassar jährlich um die 31 000 Euro. Allerdings gibt es zahlreiche Darlehen und Stipendien, um die man sich bewerben kann.

info

54   **For Services Rendered**

über ...
jammerten

auf der Kippe

aufgestapelt •
Haufen

durchzublättern

konzentriert •
Wasserkessel

Yet, out of the dozens of patients who whined about minor dissatisfactions, here came Patsy Randolph, a truly desperate patient: a woman telling him about ghosts, about her husband trying to drive her insane, a woman clearly on the brink.

A patient, at last, who would give Harry a chance to redeem his life.

That night he didn't bother with dinner. He came home and went straight into his den, where sat stacked in high piles a year's worth of professional journals that he'd never bothered to read since they dealt with serious psychiatric issues and didn't much affect the patients in his practice. He kicked his shoes off and began sifting through them, taking notes. He found Internet sites devoted to psychotic behavior and he spent hours online, downloading articles that could help him with Patsy's situation.

Harry was rereading an obscure article in the *Journal of Psychoses*, which he'd been thrilled to find – it was the key to dealing with her case – when he sat up, hearing a shrill whistle. He'd been so preoccupied ... Had he forgotten he'd put on the tea kettle for coffee? But then he glanced out the window and realized that

---

Übung 28   Ersetzen Sie die blau markierten Wörter durch gleichbedeutende Wörter oder Wendungen aus dem Text.

1. A lot of patients complained about minor problems.
2. He'd never made an effort to read all the journals.
3. He found Internet sites dealing with psychotic behavior.
4. He was reading an article in the 'Journal of Psychoses' again which he'd been extremely pleased to find.
5. He looked out of the window and noticed that it wasn't the kettle at all.
6. Patsy's clothes weren't ironed.

For Services Rendered 55

it wasn't the kettle at all. The sound was from a bird sitting on a branch nearby, singing. The hour was well past dawn.

At her next session Patsy looked worse than she had the week before. Her clothes weren't pressed. Her hair was matted and hadn't been shampooed for days, it seemed. Her white blouse was streaked with dirt and the collar was torn, as was her skirt. There were runs in her stockings. Only her makeup was carefully done.
'Hello, Doctor,' she said in a soft voice. She sounded timid.
'Hi, Patsy, come on in … No, not the couch today. Sit across from me.'
She hesitated. 'Why?'
'I think we'll postpone our usual work and deal with this crisis. About the voices. I'd like to see you face-to-face.'
'Crisis,' she repeated the word warily as she sat in the comfortable armchair across from his desk. She crossed her arms, looked out the window – these were all body-language messages that Harry recognized well. They meant she was nervous and defensive.

gebügelt •
verfilzt

Laufmaschen

misstrauisch

---

7. Her hair hadn't been washed for days.

8. Patsy sounded shy.

9. Harry suggested delaying their usual work.

10. Harry wanted to deal with the crisis directly.

11. Patsy sat in the armchair opposite his desk.

56 For Services Rendered

'Now, what's been happening since I saw you last?' he
asked.

She told him. There'd been more voices – her husband
kept pretending to be the ghost of her father, whispering terrible things to her. What, Harry asked, had the
ghost said? She answered: what a bad daughter she'd

oberflächlich   been, what a terrible wife she was now, what a shallow
friend. Why didn't she just kill herself and quit bring-
ing pain to everyone's life?

Harry jotted a note. 'Did it sound like your father's
voice? The tone, I mean?'

'Not my *father*,' she said, her voice cracking with
anger. 'It was my *husband*, pretending to be my father.
I told you that.'

Timbre   'I know. But the sound? The timbre?'

She thought. 'Maybe. But my husband had met him.
And there are videos of dad. Peter must've heard them

imitiert   and impersonated him.'

'Where was Peter when you heard him?'

schaute sich ...   She studied a bookshelf. 'He wasn't exactly home.'
genauer an •   'He wasn't?'

installiert •   'No. He went out for cigarettes. But I figured out how
Lautsprecher   he did it. He must've rigged up some kind of a speaker

---

Übung 29   Bilden Sie zu den folgenden Antworten Fragesätze mit den
Fragewörtern what, who, where, how. Es gibt meist mehrere
Lösungen.

1. Patsy's husband was whispering terrible things to her.

2. It was Patsy's husband pretending to be her father.

3. Patsy thought that maybe the timbre was her father's.

4. Patsy studied a bookshelf.

5. Peter had gone out for cigarettes.

6. Patsy cleared her throat.

and tape recorder. Or maybe one of those walkie-talkie things.' Her voice faded. 'Peter's also a good mimic. You know, doing impersonations. So he could do *all* the voices.'

'*All* of them?'

She cleared her throat. 'There were more ghosts this time.' Her voice rising again, manically. 'My grandfather. My mother. Others. I don't even know who.' Patsy stared at him for a moment then looked down. She clicked her purse latch compulsively, then looked inside, took out her compact and lipstick. She stared at the makeup, put it away. Her hands were shaking.

Harry waited a long moment. 'Patsy … I want to ask you something.'

'You can ask me anything, Doctor.'

'Just assume – for the sake of argument – that Peter wasn't pretending to be the ghosts. Where else could they be coming from?'

She snapped, 'You don't believe a word of this, do you?'

The most difficult part of being a therapist is making sure your patients know you're on their side, while you continue pursuing the truth. He said evenly, 'It's cer-

Imitator •
Stimmen nach-
ahmen

räusperte sich

Verschluss •
Puderdose

fuhr ihn an

nachzugehen •
gelassen

7. Patsy clicked her purse latch compulsively.

8. Harry waited a long moment.

9. Harry asked Patsy to assume that Peter wasn't pretending to be the ghosts.

10. The most difficult part of being a therapist is making sure your patients know you're on their side.

58 **For Services Rendered**

das vergessen

tainly possible – what you're saying about your husband. But let's put that aside and consider that there's another reason for the voices.'

'Which is?'

'That you did hear something – maybe your husband on the phone, maybe the TV, maybe the radio, but whatever it was had nothing to do with ghosts. You projected your own thoughts onto what you heard.'

'You're saying it's all in my head.'

ihren Ursprung
haben in

'I'm saying that maybe the words themselves are originating in your subconscious. What do you think about that?'

She considered this for a moment. 'I don't know … It could be. I suppose that makes some sense.'

Harry smiled. 'That's good, Patsy. That's a good first step, admitting that.'

zufrieden

She seemed pleased, a student who'd been given a gold star by a teacher.

wurde

Then the psychiatrist grew serious. 'Now, one thing: When the voices talk about your hurting yourself … you're not going to listen to them, are you?'

'No, I won't.' She offered a brave smile. 'Of course not.'

Übung 30   Verstehen Sie die blau markierten Wörter und Wendungen?
Jeweils eine der drei Erklärungen dazu ist richtig.
Kreuzen Sie sie an.

1. Harry suggested that Patsy projected her own thoughts onto what she heard.

He suggested that Patsy wrongly imagined what she heard.
He suggested that Patsy heard herself speaking.
He suggested that Patsy was only dreaming.

For Services Rendered 59

'Good.' He glanced at the clock. 'I see our time's just about up, Patsy. I want you to do something. I want you to keep a diary of what the voices say to you.'

darüber Tagebuch führen

'A diary? All right.'

'Write down everything they say and we'll go through it together.'

She rose. Turned to him. 'Maybe I should just ask one of the ghosts to come along to a session ... But then you'd have to charge me double, wouldn't you?'

berechnen

He laughed. 'See you next week.'

At three A.M. the next morning Harry was wakened by a phone call.

'Dr. Bernstein?'

'Yes?'

'I'm Officer Kavanaugh with the police department.'

Sitting up, trying to shake off his drowsiness, he thought immediately of Herb, a patient at the clinic in Brooklyn.

Schläfrigkeit

The poor man, a mild schizophrenic who was completely harmless, was forever getting beat up because of his gruff, threatening manner.

wurde ... zusammengeschlagen •

barsch

2. Patsy was like a student who'd been given a gold star by a teacher.
  She was like a student who had received a bar of gold.
  She was like a student who had been given a good grade.
  She was like a student who'd received an award.

3. Patsy asked Harry whether he would have to charge her double.
  Patsy asked Harry whether he would be extra annoyed with her.
  Patsy wondered whether Harry would ask for twice his regular fee.
  Patsy wondered whether she would have to pay for two hours.

60 **For Services Rendered**

But that wasn't the reason for the call.

'You're Mrs. Patricia Randolph's psychiatrist. Is that correct?'

pochte   His heart thudded hard. 'Yes, I am. Is she all right?'

'We've had a call ... We found her in the street outside her apartment. No one's hurt but she's a bit hysterical.'

'I'll be right there.'

When he arrived at the Randolphs' apartment building, ten blocks away, Harry found Patsy and her husband in the front lobby. A uniformed policeman stood next to them.

Harry knew that the Randolphs were wealthy but the building was much nicer than he'd expected.

Penthousewoh-   It was one of the luxurious high-rises that Donald
nungen über   Trump had built in the eighties. There were penthouse
drei Etagen   triplexes selling for \$20 million, Harry had read in the *Times*.

Übertragung •   'Doctor,' Patsy cried when she saw Harry. She ran to
   him. Harry was careful about physical contact with his
Gegen-   patients. He knew all about transference and counter-
übertragung   transference – the perfectly normal attraction between

---

Übung 31   Setzen Sie das eingeklammerte Adjektiv je nach Textumfeld in eine der beiden Steigerungsformen (Komparativ oder Superlativ). Beispiel: The building was _____ (nice) than he'd expected. Die Lösung ist nicer.

1. Her heart was thudding _____ (hard) than ever before.

2. Patsy was _____ (hysterical) than he had imagined she would be.

3. The Randolph's apartment building was _____ (far) away than Harry thought.

patients and their therapists – but contact had to be handled carefully. Harry took Patsy by the shoulders so that she couldn't hug him and led her back to the lobby couch.

'Mr. Randolph?' Harry asked, turning to her husband.

'That's right.'

'I'm Harry Bernstein.'

The men shook hands. Peter Randolph was very much what Harry was expecting. He was a trim, athletic man of about forty. Handsome. His eyes were angry and bewildered and looked victimized. He reminded Harry of a patient he'd treated briefly – a man whose sole complaint was that he was having trouble maintaining a life with a wife and two mistresses. Peter wore a burgundy silk bathrobe and supple leather slippers.

'Would you mind if I spoke to Patsy alone?' Harry asked him.

'No. I'll be upstairs if you need me.' He said this to both Harry and the police officer.

Harry too glanced at the cop, who also stepped away and let the doctor talk to his patient.

'What happened?' Harry asked Patsy.

'The bird,' she said, choking back tears.

*gepflegt •
verwirrt • als ob
er sich unge-
recht behandelt
fühlte • einzig*

weich

4. Patsy Randolph was among the _____ (wealthy) clients Harry had.

5. It might be one of the _____ (luxurious) high-rises in the area.

6. Harry was aware that a therapist's contact with his patients had to be handled _____ (carefully) than with other people.

7. Peter Randolph might well be the _____ (trim) and _____ (athletic) man Harry had ever seen.

8. Peter Randolph was _____ (angry) than Harry had imagined and also _____ (bewildered) than Harry had ever seen a man.

9. You couldn't find _____ (supple) leather slippers in all New York.

62 For Services Rendered

'One of the ceramic birds?'

'Yes,' she whispered. 'He broke it.'

strähnig

Harry studied her carefully. She was in bad shape tonight. Hair stringy, robe filthy, fingernails unclean. As in her session the other day, only her makeup was normal.

'Tell me about what happened.'

'I was asleep and then I heard this voice say, 'Run! You have to get out. They're almost here. They're going to hurt you.' And I jumped out of bed and ran into the living room and there – there was the Boehm bird. The

Rotkehlchen

robin. It was shattered and scattered all over the floor. I started screaming – because I knew they were after me.' Her voice rose. 'The ghosts … They … I mean, *Peter* was after me. I just threw on my robe and escaped.'

'And what did Peter do?'

'He ran after me.'

'But he didn't hurt you?'

marmorn

She hesitated. 'No.' She looked around the cold, marble lobby with paranoid eyes. 'Well, what he did was he called the police … But don't you see? Peter didn't have any choice. He *had* to call the police. Isn't that what somebody would normally do if their wife ran out

---

Übung 32   Welches Wort passt in die Lücke? Orientieren Sie sich am Text und ordnen Sie okay, help, leave, carpet, dirty zu.

1. Patsy's hair was _____.

2. Her makeup looked _____.

3. The lobby had no _____.

4. Peter had called for _____.

5. The ghosts told Patsy to _____.

For Services Rendered 63

of the apartment screaming? *Not* calling them would have been suspicious …' Her voice faded.

Harry looked for signs of overmedication or drinking. He could see none. She looked around the lobby once more.

'Are you feeling better now?'

She nodded. 'I'm sorry,' she said. 'Making you come all the way over here tonight.'

'That's what I'm here for … Tell me: You don't hear any voices now, do you?'

'No.'

'And the bird? Could it have been an accident?'

She thought about this for a moment. 'Well, Peter *was* asleep … Maybe I was looking at it earlier and left it on the edge of the table.' She sounded perfectly reasonable. 'Maybe the housekeeper did. I *might've* bumped it.'

The policeman looked at his watch and then ambled over. He asked, 'Can I talk to you, doctor?'

They stepped into a corner of the lobby.

'I'm thinking I oughta take her downtown,' the cop said in a Queens drawl. 'She was pretty outta control before. But it's your call. You think she's ED*?'

verebbte • Einnahme zu vieler Medikamente

Haushälterin • dagegengestoßen • schlenderte herüber

in schleppendem Queens-Akzent • Entscheidung

In der englischen Umgangssprache werden viele Abkürzungen verwendet. So bedeutet „ED" „emotionally disturbed", deutsch „seelisch gestört". Für was stehen die folgenden Abkürzungen? Kreuzen Sie die richtige Lösung an.

Übung 33

1. AC	air conditioning	aircraft
2. ID	independent driver	identity card
3. PC	politically correct	police car
4. TV	televised	television
5. ER	emergency room	Elvis Revival

64   For Services Rendered

auslösend •
Zwangseinwei-
sung • ins Kran-
kenhaus einge-
wiesen werden

Emotionally disturbed – the trigger diagnosis for involuntary commitment. If he said, yes, Patsy would be taken off and hospitalized.

This was the critical moment. Harry debated.

I can help you and you can help me …

He said to the cop, 'Give me a minute.'

He returned to Patsy, sat down next to her. 'We have a problem. The police want to take you to a hospital. And if you claim that Peter's trying to drive you crazy or hurt you, the fact is the judge just isn't going to believe you.'

'Me? *I'm* not doing anything! It's the voices! It's them … I mean, it's Peter.'

'But they're not going to believe you. That's just the way it is. Now, you can go back upstairs and carry on with your life or they can take you downtown to the city hospital. And you don't want that. Believe me. Can you stay in control?'

sich unter Kont-
rolle halten

She lowered her head to her hands. Finally she said, 'Yes, Doctor, I can.'

'Good … Patsy, I want to ask you something else. I want to see your husband alone. Can I call him, have him come in?'

Übung 34

Vervollständigen Sie die Bedingungssätze (if-Sätze).
Welche der drei Möglichkeiten passt in die Lücke?

1. If Patsy _____ that Peter was trying to drive her crazy the judge wouldn't believe her.
   (claimed/had claimed/would claim)

2. Who knows what _____ if Patsy was hospitalized.
   (would happen/happened/would have happened)

3. Everything would be perfect if Patsy _____ in control. (stays, stayed, would stay)

For Services Rendered **65**

'Why?' she asked, her face dark with suspicion.

'Because I'm your doctor and I want to get to the bottom of what's bothering you.'

dem auf den Grund gehen will

She glanced at the cop. Gave him a dark look. Then she said to Harry, 'Sure.'

'Good.'

After Patsy'd disappeared into the elevator car the cop said, 'I don't know, doctor. She seems like a nut case to me. Things like this … they can get real ugly. I've seen it a million times.'

jemand, der ziemlich verrückt ist

'She's got some problems but she's not dangerous.'

'You're willing to take that chance?'

After a moment he said, 'Yes, I'm willing to take that chance.'

'How was she last night, after I left?' Harry asked Peter Randolph the next morning. The two men sat in Harry's office.

'She seemed all right. Calmer.' Peter sipped the coffee that Miriam had brought him. 'What exactly is going on with her?'

'I'm sorry,' Harry said, 'I can't discuss the specifics of your wife's condition with you. Confidentiality.'

Einzelheiten •
Schweigepflicht

4. Patsy _____ why Harry wanted to see her husband if she had been honest to herself.
(did know/had known/would have known)

5. If Patsy _____ like a nut case to the cop why had he not taken her to a hospital?
(had seemed/seems/would have seemed)

66 **For Services Rendered**

flackerten ... auf

Peter's eyes flared angrily for a moment. 'Then why did you ask me here?'

'Because I need you to help me treat her. You do want her to get better, don't you?'

'Of course, I do. I love her very much.' He sat forward in the chair. 'But I don't understand what's going on. She was fine until a couple of months ago – when she started seeing *you*, if you have to know the truth. Then things started to go bad.'

Themen

'When people see therapists they sometimes confront issues they've never had to deal with. I think that was Patsy's situation. She's getting close to some important issues. And that can be very disorienting.'

'She claims I'm pretending to be a ghost,' Peter said sarcastically. 'That seems a little worse than just disoriented.'

Abwärtsspirale

'She's in a downward spiral. I can pull her out of it ... but it'll be hard. And I'll need your help.'

Peter shrugged. 'What can I do?'

Harry explained, 'First of all you can be honest with

angefangen, Sie

me.'

mit ... in Verbindung zu bringen

'Of course.'

'For some reason she's come to associate you with her

Übung 35   Beantworten Sie die folgenden Fragen zum Text.
Nur eine Möglichkeit ist richtig.
Tragen Sie ein T für true oder ein F für false in die Kästchen ein.

1. What are Peter's feelings for his wife?
He loves her very much.   He hates her.
He feels indifferent towards her.

2. When did Patsy start feeling bad?
half a year ago   a few months ago   a week ago

For Services Rendered **67**

father. She has a lot of resentment toward him and she's projecting that onto you. Do you know why she's mad at you?'

hat ... negative
Gefühle für ihn

There was silence for a moment.

'Go on, tell me. Anything you say here is confidential – just between you and me.'

vertraulich

'She might have this stupid idea that I've cheated on her.'

'Have you?'

'Where the hell do you get off, asking a question like that?'

maßen Sie sich
an •

Harry said reasonably, 'I'm just trying to get to the truth.'

in ruhigem Ton

Randolph calmed down. 'No, I haven't cheated on her. She's paranoid.'

'And you haven't said or done anything that might trouble her deeply or affect her sense of reality.'

'No,' Peter said.

'How much is she worth?' Harry asked bluntly.

geradeheraus •

Peter blinked. 'You mean, her portfolio?'

Anlagevermö-

'Net worth.'

gen

'I don't know exactly. About eleven million.'

Harry nodded. 'And the money's all hers, isn't it?'

3. Does Harry think he can help Patsy?

   no   yes   maybe

4. How does Patsy feel towards her father?

   She doesn't like him.   She is angry at him.
   She misses him.

5. Peter thinks he knows why Patsy is upset.

   She thinks Peter wants to move out.
   She thinks Peter wants to divorce her.
   She thinks Peter has cheated on her.

68 For Services Rendered

A frown crossed Peter Randolph's face. 'What're you asking?'

'I'm asking, if Patsy were to go insane or to kill herself would you get her money?'

'Go to hell!' Randolph shouted, standing up quickly. For a moment Harry thought the man was going to hit him. But he pulled his wallet from his hip pocket and took out a card. Tossed it onto Harry's desk. 'That's our lawyer. Call him and ask him about the prenuptial agreement. If Patricia's declared insane or if she were to die the money goes into a trust. I don't get a penny.'

Harry pushed the card back. 'That won't be necessary. I'm sorry if I hurt your feelings,' Harry said. 'My patient's care comes before everything else. I had to know there's no motive for harming her.'

Randolph adjusted his cuffs and buttoned his jacket. 'Accepted.'

Harry nodded and looked Peter Randolph over carefully. A prerequisite for being a therapist is the ability to judge character quickly. He now sized up this man and came to a decision. 'I want to try something radical with Patsy and I want you to help me.'

'Radical? You mean commit her?'

Stirnrunzeln — frown
warf — Tossed
Ehevertrag — prenuptial agreement
Stiftung — trust
Manschetten — cuffs
Grundvoraussetzung — prerequisite
schätzte ... ab — sized up
in eine Anstalt einweisen — commit

Übung 36 Finden Sie die im folgenden Text versteckten sechs sachlichen Fehler.

Harry asked Patsy's brother about her financial situation. First Peter got angry at Harry but eventually he calmed down and explained about the agreement he and Patsy had before they got married. If Penelope (Patsy was just a nickname) didn't love him anymore he would get all the money. Harry apologized to Peter and explained to him that he needed his help. However Peter refused. He was jealous of Harry.

For Services Rendered **69**

'No, that'd be the worst thing for her. When patients are going through times like this you can't coddle them. You have to be tough. And force *them* to be tough.'

umsorgen

'Meaning?'

'Don't be antagonistic but force her to stay involved in life. She's going to want to withdraw – to be pampered. But don't spoil her. If she says she's too upset to go shopping or go out to dinner, don't let her get away with it. Insist that she does what she's supposed to do.'

verhalten Sie sich ihr gegenüber nicht feindselig • zurückziehen • verwöhnen

'You're sure that's best?'

Sure? Harry asked himself. No, he wasn't the least bit sure. But he'd made his decision. He had to push Patsy hard. He told Peter, 'We don't have any choice.'

But after the man left the office Harry happened to recall an expression one of his medical school professors had used frequently. He said you have to attack disease head-on. *'You have to kill or cure.'*

erinnerte sich ...
an •
direkt

Harry hadn't thought of that expression in years. He wished he hadn't today.

The next day Patsy walked into his office without an appointment.

Welche Wörter passen in die Lücken? Entscheiden Sie sich für eine der angegebenen Möglichkeiten.

Übung 37

1. Harry thinks that patients need a _____ hand.
(loving, strong, weak)

2. Harry tells Peter not to _____ Patsy. (hit, spoil, kiss)

3. Harry was a very _____ psychiatrist.
(boring, indifferent, passionate)

4. One of his professor's expressions had been that you have to kill or to _____ . (give up, heal, hope)

5. Patsy came to see Harry without having _____ an appointment. (changed, arranged, canceled)

70 For Services Rendered

der Normalfall

In Brooklyn, at the clinic, this was standard procedure and nobody thought anything of it.

eines Seelen-
klempners •
Spontansitzun-
gen • bauschte
... auf

But in a Park Avenue shrink's office impromptu sessions were taboo. Still Harry could see from her face that she was very upset and he didn't make an issue of her unexpected appearance.

She collapsed on the couch and hugged herself closely as he rose and closed the door.

'Patsy, what's the matter?' he asked.

He noticed that her clothes were more disheveled than he'd ever seen. They were stained and torn. Hair

ungepflegt •

bedraggled. Fingernails dirty.

schluchzte

'Everything was going so well,' she sobbed, 'then I was sitting in the den early this morning and I heard my father's ghost again. He said, 'They're almost here. You don't have much time left ...' And I asked, 'What do you mean?' And he said, 'Look in the living room.' And I did and there was another one of my birds! It was shattered!' She opened her purse and showed Harry the broken pieces of ceramic. 'Now, there's only one left! I'm going to die when it breaks. I know I am. Peter's going to break it tonight! And then he'll kill me.'

Übung 38

Ordnen Sie jedem Satz eine der eingeklammerten Präpositionen zu.
Beispiel: Nobody thought anything _____ it. (on, at, of)
Die Lösung ist of.

1. Harry expected _____ his patients that they made an appointment with his receptionist. (for, of, by)
2. He could see that Patsy was very upset _____ something. (over, on, about)
3. Harry could tell that Patsy's fingernails hadn't been cleaned _____ ages. (in, at, from)

For Services Rendered **71**

'He's not going to kill you, Patsy.' Harry said calmly, patiently ignoring her hysteria.

'I think I should go to the hospital for a while, Doctor.'

Harry got up and sat on the couch next to her. He took her hand. 'No.'

'What?'

'It would be a mistake,' Harry said.

'Why?' she cried.

'Because you can't hide from these issues. You have to confront them.'

'I'd feel safer in a hospital. Nobody'd try to kill me in the hospital.'

'Nobody's going to kill you, Patsy. You have to believe me.'

'No! Peter – '

'But Peter's never tried to hurt you, has he?'

A pause. 'No.'

'Okay, here's what I want you to do. Listen to me. Are you listening?'

'Yes.'

'You know that whether Peter was pretending to say those words to you or you were imagining them *they weren't real*. Repeat that.'

4. Normally Harry avoided physical contact with his patients but _____ this session he felt it was okay to sit next to Pasty. (at, on, during)

5. Patsy wanted Harry to admit her _____ hospital but he refused. (into, to, onto)

6. Harry asked Patsy to repeat _____ him that she was just imagining things. (at, after, on)

72   **For Services Rendered**

'I –'

'Repeat it!'

'They weren't real.'

'Now say, 'There was no ghost. My father's dead.''

'There was no ghost. My father's dead.'

'Good!' Harry laughed. 'Again.'

Mantra • She repeated this mantra several times, calming each

ging ... über time. Finally a faint smile crossed her lips. Then she
frowned. 'But the bird ...' She again opened her purse

und hielt ... fest and took out the shattered ceramic, cradling the
pieces in her trembling hand.

'Whatever happened to the bird doesn't matter. It's
only a piece of porcelain.'

Scherben 'But ...' she looked down at the broken shards.

Harry leaned forward. 'Listen to me, Patsy. Listen
carefully.' Passionately the doctor said, 'I want you

ihn mit aller to go home, take that last bird and smash the hell out

Kraft zertrüm- of it.'

mern 'You want me to ...'

'Take a hammer and crush it.'

She started to protest but then she smiled. 'Can I do
that?'

'You bet you can. Just give yourself permission to. Go

Übung 39   Ersetzen Sie die blau markierten Wörter durch gleichbedeutende
Wörter oder Wendungen aus dem Text.

1. Patsy kept saying that there was no ghost and that her
   father was dead and every time she did she found she
   relaxed a bit more.
2. Harry told Patsy to break the last bird into pieces with all
   her might.
3. He reassured her that she could do it and that she should
   allow herself to do it.

For Services Rendered 73

home, have a nice glass of wine, find a hammer and
smash it.' He reached under his desk and picked up the
wastebasket. He held it out for her. 'They're just pieces
of china, Patsy.'   Porzellan
After a moment she tossed the pieces of the statue into
the container.
'Good, Patsy.' And – thinking, the hell with transfer-   zur Hölle mit
ence – the doctor gave his patient a huge hug.

That evening Patsy Randolph returned home and
found Peter sitting in front of the television.
'You're late,' he said. 'Where've you been?'
'Out shopping. I got a bottle of wine.'
'We're supposed to go to Jack and Louise's tonight.
Don't tell me you forgot.'
'I don't feel like,' she said. 'I don't feel well. I –'
'No. We're going. You're not getting out of it.'   Davor wirst du
                                                              dich nicht drü-
He spoke in that same weird abrupt tone he'd been   cken.
using for the past week.
'Well, can I at least take care of a few things first?'
'Sure. But I don't want to be late.'
Patsy walked into the kitchen, opened a bottle

4. Harry didn't care anymore about the fact that he shouldn't
hug his patients.
5. Peter told Patsy that they had made plans to visit their
friends that evening.
6. Patsy replied that she didn't want to go.
7. However he told her she couldn't avoid going.
8. In the end Patsy said that she needed to do a few things first.

74 For Services Rendered

of the expensive Merlot and poured a large glass just like Dr. Bernstein had told her. She sipped it. She felt good. Very good. 'Where's the hammer?' she called.

'Hammer? What do you need the hammer for?'

in Ordnung bringen

'I have to fix something.'

'I think it's in the drawer beside the refrigerator.'

She found it. Carried it into the living room. She glanced at the last Boehm bird, an owl.

Peter looked at the tool, then back to the TV. 'What do you have to fix?'

stumpf

'You,' she answered and brought the blunt end down on the top of his head with all her strength.

It took another dozen blows to kill him and when she'd finished she stood back and gazed at the re-markable patterns the blood made on the carpet and couch. Then she went into the bedroom and picked up her diary from the bedside table – the one Dr. Bern-stein had suggested she keep. Back in the living room Patsy sat down beside her husband's corpse and

weitschweifig

she wrote a rambling passage in the booklet about how, at last, she'd gotten the ghosts to stop speak-ing to her. She was finally at peace. She didn't add

---

Übung 40   Welche der folgenden Aussagen stimmen?
Tragen Sie ein T für true oder ein F für false in die Kästchen ein.

1. Patsy was in a bad mood when she poured herself a glass of wine.

2. Peter Randolph didn't realize that his wife was going to kill him.

3. Patsy didn't stop hitting Peter with the hammer until he was dead.

4. She was shaking all over when she made an entry about what had happened in her diary.

For Services Rendered   **75**

as much as she wanted to; it was very time-consuming to write using your finger for a pen and blood for ink.

zeitraubend •
als

When Patsy'd finished she picked up the hammer and smashed the Boehm ceramic owl into dust.

Then she began screaming as loudly as she could: 'The ghosts are dead, the ghosts are dead, the ghosts are dead!'

Long before she was hoarse the police and medics arrived. When they took her away she was wearing a straightjacket.

Zwangsjacke

A week later Harry Bernstein sat in the prison hospital waiting room. He knew he was a sight – he hadn't shaved in several days and was wearing wrinkled clothes – which in fact he'd slept in last night. He stared at the filthy floor.

kein schöner
Anblick • zer-
knittert

'You all right?' This question came from a tall, thin man with a perfect beard. He wore a gorgeous suit and Armani-framed glasses. He was Patsy's lead defense lawyer.

eine Brille mit
...-Gestell •
Hauptverteidi-
ger

'I never thought she'd do it,' Harry said to him. 'I *knew*

5. The neighbors heard her crying and called an ambulance as they were worried about her.

6. The last time Harry had seen Patsy was when he had told her to smash the last bird with a hammer.

7. Patsy's lawyer looked perfect whilst Harry looked terrible.

76 For Services Rendered

there was risk. I *knew* something was wrong. But I thought I had everything under control.'

The lawyer looked at him sympathetically. 'I heard you've been having some trouble too. Your patients …'

in Scharen •
gibt es wie Sand
am Meer

Harry laughed bitterly. 'Are quitting in droves. Well, wouldn't you? Park Avenue shrinks are a dime a dozen. Why should they risk seeing me? I might get them killed or committed.'

Gefängnis-
beamte •

The jailor opened the door. 'Dr. Bernstein, you can see the prisoner now.'

und stützte sich
am … ab •

He stood slowly, supporting himself on the door frame.

musterte ihn •
angehen •
Unzurechnungs-
fähigkeit

The lawyer looked him over and said, 'You and I can meet in the next couple days to decide how to handle the case. The insanity defense is tough in New York but with you on board I can make it work. We'll keep her out of jail … Say, doctor, you going to be okay?'

Harry gave a shallow nod.

Sachverständi-
genhonorar

The lawyer said kindly, 'I can arrange for a little cash for you. A couple thousand – for an expert witness fee.'

'Thanks,' Harry said. But he instantly forgot about the money. His mind was already on his patient.

Übung 41   Verlaufsform oder Grundform? Nach bestimmten Verben folgt entweder die Verlaufsform oder die Grundform. Beispiel: Why should they risk seeing Harry? Setzen Sie die Verben in die richtigen Formen.

1. Patsy's lawyer couldn't help _____ (think) that something was wrong with Harry.

2. He suggested _____ (meet) Harry to discuss how they were going to handle Patsy's case.

3. He hoped _____ (find) a way to help Patsy.

For Services Rendered   **77**

The room was as bleak as he'd expected.   trostlos •

Face white, eyes shrunken, Patsy lay in bed, looking   eingesunken
out the window. She glanced at Harry, didn't seem to
recognize him.

'How are you feeling?' he asked.

'Who are you?' She frowned.

He didn't answer her question either. 'You're not looking too bad, Patsy.'

'I think I know you. Yes, you're … Wait, are you a
ghost?'

'No, I'm not a ghost.' Harry set his attaché case   Aktenkoffer •
on the table. Her eyes slipped to the case as he opened   wanderten zu
it.

'I can't stay long, Patsy. I'm closing my practice.
There's a lot to take care of. But I wanted to bring you a
few things.'

'Things?' she asked, sounding like a child. 'For me?
Like Christmas. Like my birthday.'

'Uh-hum.' Harry rummaged in the case. 'Here's the   wühlte in
first thing.' He took out a photocopy. 'It's an article in
the *Journal of Psychoses*. I found it the night after the
session when you first told me about the ghosts. You
should read it.'

4. Patsy obviously wanted to avoid _____ (spend)
the rest of her life in jail.

5. The lawyer offered _____ (help out) Harry with a
few thousand dollars.

6. When Harry went into Patsy's room she didn't seem
_____ (recognize) him.

7. She used to like _____ (talk) to Harry during their
sessions.

8. When Patsy started _____ (talk) about ghosts Harry
got slightly impatient.

'I can't read,' she said. 'I don't know how.' She gave a crazy laugh. 'I'm afraid of the food here. I think there are spies around. They're going to put things in the food. Disgusting things. And poison. Or broken glass.' Another cackle.

Harry set the article on the bed next to her. He walked to the window. No trees here. No birds. Just gray, downtown Manhattan.

He said, glancing back at her, 'It's all about ghosts. The article.'

beherrschte

Her eyes narrowed and then fear consumed her face.

'Ghosts,' she whispered. 'Are there ghosts here?'

Harry laughed hard. 'See, Patsy, ghosts were the first

Hinweis •

clue. After you mentioned them in that session –

behauptend

claiming that your husband was driving you crazy – I thought something didn't sound quite right. So I went

zu recherchieren

home and started to research your case.'

She gazed at him silently.

'That article's about the importance of diagnosis in

die Versiche-

mental health cases. See, sometimes it works to some-

rungsschadens-

body's advantage to *appear* to be mentally unstable –

ansprüche vor-

so they can avoid responsibility. Say, soldiers who

täuschen

don't want to fight. People faking insurance claims.

Übung 42

Was ist die richtige Antwort auf die folgenden Fragen? Tragen Sie ein T für true oder ein F für false in die Kästchen ein.

1. How does Patsy feel?

        unhappy   scared   confused

2. What was the article about that Harry had found?

        hallucinations   insanity   diagnosis

3. Where was Patsy?

        in a prison cell   in a prison hospital

        in a prison's psychiatric ward.

For Services Rendered 79

People who've committed crimes.' He turned back. 'Or who're *about to* commit a crime.'

kurz davorstehen

'I'm afraid of ghosts,' Patsy said, her voice rising. 'I'm afraid of ghosts. I don't want any ghosts here! I'm afraid of – '

Harry continued like a lecturing professor. 'And ghosts are one of the classic hallucinations that sane people use to try to convince other people that they're insane.'

Professor, der eine Vorlesung hält • gesund

Patsy closed her mouth.

'Fascinating article,' Harry continued, nodding toward it. 'See, ghosts and spirits *seem* like the products of delusional minds. But in fact they're complex metaphysical concepts that someone who's really insane wouldn't understand at all. No, true psychotics believe that the actual *person* is there speaking to them. They think that Napoleon or Hitler or Marilyn Monroe is really in the room with them. You wouldn't have claimed to've heard your father's *ghost*. You would actually have heard *him*.'

wahnsinnig

Harry enjoyed the utterly shocked expression on his patient's face. He said, 'Then, a few weeks ago, you admitted that maybe the voices were in your head. A

völlig

Finden und korrigieren Sie die im Text versteckten sechs grammatischen Fehler.

Übung 43

Harry didn't believe what Patsy were telling him. On the contrary he thought she was a well actress and was actually trying to deceive himself. However Patsy kept talking about ghost and how she was afraid of them. She told Harry people wants to kill her. She finally stopped when Harry told her in detail about the article he had founded and how he believed she was making it all up.

true psychotic would never admit that. They'd swear they were completely sane.' He paced slowly. 'There were some other things too. You must've read somewhere that *sloppy* physical appearance is a sign of mental illness. Your clothes were torn and dirty, you'd forget *to do straps* … but your makeup was always perfect – even on the night the police called me over to your apartment. In genuine mental health cases makeup is the first thing to go. Patients just *smear their faces with it*. Has to do with issues of masking their identity, if you're interested.

'Oh, and remember? You asked if a ghost could come to one of our sessions? That was very funny. But the psychiatric literature defines humor as ironic *juxtaposition* of concepts based on common experience. Of course that's contrary to the mental processes of psychotics.'

'What the hell does that mean?' Patsy spat out.

'That crazy people don't make jokes,' *he summarized*. '*That cinched it for me* that you were sane as could be.' Harry looked through the attaché case once more. 'Next …' He looked up, smiling. 'After I read that article and decided you were faking your diagnosis – and

schlampig

die Riemen zuzumachen

schmieren es sich in ihre Gesichter

Nebeneinanderstellung

fasste er zusammen • damit war es für mich glasklar

Übung 44

Setzen Sie das richtige Relativpronomen in die Sätze ein. Wählen Sie zwischen *who*, *that*, *whose*, *whom*.

1. The clothes _____ Patsy was wearing were torn and dirty.
2. The ghosts _____ Patsy kept mentioning didn't exist.
3. People _____ minds are disturbed don't make jokes.
4. The literature _____ Harry had read dealt with psychotics.
5. Patients _____ are genuine mental health cases don't wear perfect makeup.
6. Patsy's father _____ she resented very much had just been used as part of her story.

For Services Rendered   **81**

listening to what your subconscious was telling me about your marriage – I figured you were using me for some reason having to do with your husband. So I hired a private eye.'

'Jesus Christ, you did what?'

'Here's his report.' He dropped the folder on the bed. 'It says basically that your husband *was* having an affair and was forging checks on your main investment account. You knew about his mistress and the money and you'd talked to a lawyer about divorcing him. But Peter knew that *you* were having an affair too – with your friend Sally's husband. Peter used that to blackmail you into not divorcing him.'

Patsy stared at him, frozen.

He nodded at the report. 'Oh, you may as well look at it. Pretending you can't read? Doesn't fly*. Reading has nothing to do with psychotic behavior: it's a developmental and IQ issue.'

She opened the report, read through it then tossed it aside disgustedly. 'Son of a bitch.'

Harry said, 'You wanted to kill Peter and you wanted me to establish that you were insane – for your defense. You'd go into a private hospital. There'd be a

Privatdetektiv

Mappe

fälschte • Anlagekonto • sich von ihm scheiden zu lassen

erpressen • mit versteinerter Miene • Das zieht nicht. • Frage der Entwicklung und Intelligenz

Redewendungen gehören zum ständigen Sprachgebrauch und können nicht immer vom wörtlichen Sinn abgeleitet werden. Harry meint zu Patsy: „Doesn't fly" = „Es zieht nicht", als sie wieder behauptet, sie könne nicht lesen. Andere Redewendungen, die das Fliegen aufgreifen, sind „to fly by the seats of one's pants", etwas mit links machen, und „to fly the flag", was bedeutet, dass jemand sehr patriotisch ist und im wörtlichen Sinn auch, wie viele Amerikaner, die Flagge vor dem Haus hisst. Wenn jemand sagt „pigs might fly", dann meint er „wer's glaubt, wird selig".

info

82   **For Services Rendered**

vorgeschriebene
Wiederanhörung

provozieren

ungenau

mandatory rehearing in a year and, bang, you'd pass the tests and be released.'

She shook her head. 'But you knew my goal was to kill Peter? And you let me do it! Hell, you *encouraged* me to do it.'

'And when I saw Peter I encouraged *him* to **antagonize** you … It was time to move things along. I was getting tired of our sessions.' Then Harry's face darkened with genuine regret. 'I never thought you'd actually kill him, just assault him. But, hey, what can I say? Psychiatry's an **inexact** science.'

'But why didn't you go to the police?' she said, whispering, close to panic.

'Ah, that has to do with the third thing I brought for you.'

I can help you and you can help me …

He lifted an envelope out of his briefcase. He handed it to her.

'What is this?'

'My bill.'

She opened it. Took out the sheet of paper.

At the top was written '*For Services Rendered*.' And below that: '*$10 million*.'

Übung 45   Setzen Sie die unregelmäßigen Verben in die angegebene Zeitform.

1. Patsy admitted to Harry it _____ her goal to kill her husband. (be – past perfect)

2. She was shocked though that he _____ about it all the time. (know – past perfect)

3. Before visiting Patsy Harry _____ a bill that he was going to give to her. (write – past tense)

4. He _____ her a million dollars so she would be able to pay her lawyer. (leave – past tense)

For Services Rendered **83**

'Are you crazy?' Patsy gasped.

Given the present location and context of their conversation, Harry had to laugh at her choice of words. 'Peter was nice enough to tell me exactly what you were worth. I'm leaving you a million … which you'll probably need to pay that slick lawyer of yours. He looks expensive. Now, I'll need cash or a certified check before I testify at your trial. Otherwise I'll have to share with the court my honest diagnosis about your condition.'

'You're blackmailing me!'

'I guess I am.'

'Why?'

'Because with this money I can afford to do some good. And help people who really need helping.' He nodded at bill. 'I'd write that check pretty soon – they have the death penalty in New York now. Oh, and by the way, I'd lose that bit about the food being poisoned. Around here if you make a stink about meals, they'll just put you on a tube.' He picked up his attaché case.

'Wait,' she begged. 'Don't leave! Let's talk about this!'

'Sorry.' Harry nodded at a wall clock. 'I see our time is up.'

stieß … hervor •
angesichts

Bargeld •
gedeckter
Scheck • aussa-
ge

wegen … Ärger
machen • legen
sie Ihnen eine
Magensonde

5. Harry warned Patsy that if she _____ a complaint about the food they would put her on a tube. (make – past tense)

6. First Patsy pretended she _____ not _____ anything wrong. (do – past perfect)

Without Jonathan

Marissa Cooper turned her car onto Route 232, which would take her from Portsmouth to Green Harbor, twenty miles away.

Thinking: This was the same road that she and Jonathan had taken to and from the mall a thousand times, carting back necessities, silly luxuries and occasional treasures.

Einkaufszentrum • nach Hause schleppend • notwendige Dinge •

The road near which they'd found their dream house when they'd moved to Maine seven years ago.

The road they'd taken to go to their anniversary celebration last May.

Hochzeitstagsfeier

Tonight, though, all those memories led to one place: her life without Jonathan.

The setting sun behind her, she steered through the lazy turns, hoping to lose those difficult – but tenacious – thoughts.

steuerte ... durch • hartnäckig

Beantworten Sie die folgenden Fragen zum Text.
Tragen Sie ein T für true oder ein F für false in die Kästchen ein.

Übung 46

1. In which part of the USA does Marissa Cooper live?
on the West Coast   on the East Coast

2. What had Marissa and Jonathan celebrated last May?
their birthdays   their wedding anniversary

3. Where had they driven to a thousand times?
to the shopping center   to the town center

86 Without Jonathan

Don't think about it!

Look around you, she ordered herself. Look at the rugged scenery: the slabs of purple clouds hanging over the maple and oak leaves – some gold, some red as a heart.

Scheiben •
Ahorn- und
Eichenblätter •

Look at the sunlight, a glowing ribbon draped along the dark pelt of hemlock and pine. At the absurd line of cows, walking single file in their spontaneous day-end commute back to the barn.

Pelz •
Hemlocktanne •
Kiefer • die im
Gänsemarsch
gingen • würde-
voll • versteckt

At the stately white spires of a small village, tucked five miles off the highway.

And look at you: a thirty-four-year-old woman in a spritely silver Toyota, driving fast, toward a new life.

schnittig

A life without Jonathan.

Ampel • war im
Leerlauf •
Kupplung • Satz
• Anzeige •

Twenty minutes later she came to Dannerville and braked for the first of the town's two stoplights. As her car idled, clutch in, she glanced to her right. Her heart did a little thud at what she saw.

Wartung von
Schiffsmotoren
• Becher •
Schlüsselanhän-
ger

It was a store that sold boating and fishing gear. She'd noticed in the window an ad for some kind of marine engine treatment. In this part of coastal Maine you couldn't avoid boats. They were in tourist paintings and photos, on mugs, T-shirts and key chains. And, of

---

Übung 47 Welchen Satz oder welche Textstelle umschreiben die folgenden Sätze?

1. In this part of the country everybody seemed to be crazy about boats.
2. Marissa's heart jumped a little when she saw an ad in a store window.
3. The cows were walking back to the barn one behind another just as they do at the end of every day.
4. Marissa was quite upset that the boat in the ad was just like Jonathan's boat.

Without Jonathan   87

course, there were thousands of the real things every-
where: vessels in the water, on trailers, in dry docks,
sitting in front yards – the New England version of
pick-up trucks on blocks in the rural South.
But what had struck her hard was that the boat pictured in the ad she was now looking at was a Chris-
Craft. A big one, maybe thirty-six or thirty-eight feet.
Just like Jonathan's boat. Nearly identical, in fact: the
same colors, the same configuration.
He'd bought his five years ago, and though Marissa
thought his interest in it would flag (like any boy with
a new toy), he'd proved her wrong and spent nearly
every weekend on the vessel, cruising up and down the
coast, fishing like an old cod dockhand. Her husband
would bring home to Marissa the best of his catch,
which she would clean and cook up.
Ah, Jonathan …
She swallowed hard and inhaled slowly to calm her
pounding heart. She –
A honk behind her. The stoplight had changed to
green. She drove on, trying desperately to keep her
mind from speculating about his death: The Chris-
Craft rocking unsteadily in the turbulent gray Atlantic.

Schiffe •
Trockendocks •
aufgebockt •
ländlich • ihr
einen ziem-
lichen Schlag
versetzt hatte •
Aufbau

abflauen

Dockhelfer beim
Kabeljaufang •
Fang • kochen
würde

Hupen

5. Jonathan used to fish as if he made his living from it and would
bring home what he had caught.

6. When Jonathan first got the boat Marissa had hoped that he
would soon lose interest in it.

7. What boats were for New England, trucks with an open back
were for the Southern states of the USA.

88 Without Jonathan

mit ... um sich
schlagend

fuhr gemütlich •
Ampel •
Saum

mit dem sie
gleich zu Abend
essen würde

Hin und Her

hatten sich für
... entschieden •

Kai

Jonathan overboard. His arms perhaps flailing madly, his panicked voice perhaps crying for help.

Oh, Jonathan …

Marissa cruised through Dannerville's second light and continued toward the coast. In front of her she could see, in the last of the sunlight, the skirt of the Atlantic, all that cold, deadly water.

The water responsible for life without Jonathan.

Then she told herself: No. Think about Dale instead.

Dale O'Banion, the man she was about to have dinner with in Green Harbor, the first time she'd been out with a man in a long while.

She'd met him through an ad in a magazine. They'd spoken on the phone a few times and, after considerable waltzing around on both their parts, she'd felt comfortable enough to suggest meeting in person. They'd settled on the Fishery, a popular restaurant on the wharf.

Dale had mentioned the Oceanside Café, which had better food, yes, but that was Jonathan's favorite place; she just couldn't meet Dale there.

So the Fishery it was.

She thought back to their phone conversation last

Übung 48   Welches der drei Verben passt in die Lücke? Achten Sie auch auf den umliegenden Text und kreuzen Sie die richtige Lösung an.

1. Marissa and Dale had _____ to go to a fish restaurant.

    refused   decided   wanted

2. Marissa had _____ a lot in her marriage to Jonathan.

    heard about   gone through   bought

3. Dale was the first man Marissa had _____ with in a long time.

    gone out   been seen   talked

Without Jonathan 89

night. Dale had said to her, 'I'm tall and pretty well built, little balding on top.'

ein bisschen •
schütter •
1,62 groß

'Okay, well,' she'd replied nervously, 'I'm five-five, blonde, and I'll be wearing a purple dress.'

Thinking about those words now, thinking how that simple exchange typified single life, meeting people you'd met only over the phone.

She had no problem with dating*. In fact she was looking forward to it, in a way. She'd met her husband when he was just graduating from medical school and she was twenty-one. They'd gotten engaged almost immediately; that'd been the end of her social life as a single woman. But now she'd have some fun. She'd meet interesting men, she'd begin to enjoy sex again.

machte ... seinen
Abschluss an •
hatten sich ...
verlobt

Even if it was work at first, she'd try to just relax. She'd try not to be bitter, try not to be too much of a widow.

But even as she was thinking this her thoughts went somewhere else: Would she ever actually fall in *love* again?

The way she'd once been so completely in love with Jonathan?

And would anybody love *her* completely?

Dating ist ein wichtiger Teil der amerikanischen Kultur und heißt, sich zu einem Date (also wörtlich einem bestimmten Datum) zu verabreden, auszugehen und dann im Glücksfall den passenden Partner, Freund oder die passende Freundin zu finden. Ob Schüler, Student, Erwachsener – alle ungebundenen Amerikaner und Amerikanerinnen machen beim Dating mit, es wird quasi erwartet. Man kann sich zu zweit oder auch zu einem double date mit einem anderen Paar verabreden. Manche wagen auch ein Treffen mit gänzlich Unbekannten und lassen sich auf ein blind date ein.

Without Jonathan

At another red light Marissa reached up and twisted the mirror toward her, glanced into it. The sun was now below the horizon and the light was dim, but she believed she passed the rearview-mirror test with flying colors: full lips, a wrinkle-less face reminiscent of Michelle Pfeiffer's (in a poorly-lit Toyota accessory, at least), a petite nose.

Then, too, her bod was slim and pretty firm, and, though she knew her boobs wouldn't land her on the cover of the latest Victoria's Secret catalog, she had a feeling that, in a pair of nice, tight jeans, her butt'd draw some serious attention.

At least in Portsmouth, Maine.

Hell, yes, she told herself, she'd find a man who was right for her.

Somebody who could appreciate the cowgirl within her, the girl whose Texan grandfather had taught her to ride and shoot.

Or maybe she'd find somebody who'd love her academic side – her writing and poetry and her love of teaching, which had been her job, just after college.

Or somebody who could laugh with her – at movies, at sights on the sidewalk, at funny jokes and dumb ones.

Rückspiegeltest • mit Bravour • das an ... erinnerte • schlecht beleuchtet • Zubehör • Körper • Busen • Titelseite • neueste • Hintern

seltsame Anblicke • Gehweg

Übung 49 Welche der folgenden Aussagen stimmen? Tragen Sie ein T für true oder ein F für false in die Kästchen ein.

1. Apart from her face Marissa's appearance was perfect.
2. Marissa looked great including her face.
3. Marissa had even been on the cover of a Victoria's Secret catalog.
4. She hoped to meet someone who could teach her how to ride and shoot.
5. She had learnt to ride and shoot when she was a girl and hoped to meet a real cowboy.

Without Jonathan **91**

How she loved laughing (and how little of it she'd done
lately).

in letzter Zeit

Then Marissa Cooper thought: No, wait, wait … She'd
find a man who loved *everything* about her.

But then the tears started and she pulled off the road
quickly, surrendering to the sobs.

*hielt … an •
und gab dem
Schluchzen nach*

'No, no, no …'

She forced the images of her husband out of her mind.
The cold water, the gray water …

Fives minutes later she'd calmed down. Wiped her eyes
dry, reapplied makeup and lipstick.

She drove into downtown Green Harbor and parked in
a lot near the shops and restaurants, a half block from
the wharf.

Parkplatz

A glance at the clock. It was just six-thirty. Dale O'Banion had told her that he'd be working until about seven
and would meet her at seven-thirty.

She'd come to town early to do some shopping – a little retail therapy. After that she'd go the restaurant to
wait for Dale O'Banion. But then she wondered
uneasily if it would be all right if she sat in the bar by
herself and had a glass of wine.

*Shopping-The-
rapie • unbe-
haglich*

Then she said to herself sternly, What the hell're you

ernsthaft

---

6. She hoped to meet someone who would love both her
cowgirl and her academic side or just everything about her.

7. Marissa didn't like sitting on her own in a bar.

8. She used to have a glass of wine in a bar after going
shopping.

9. Dale had told her he would meet her a couple of hours
after finishing work.

10. He had said he would come to the restaurant half an hour
after finishing work.

92 Without Jonathan

thinking? Of *course* it'd be all right. She could do anything she wanted. This was *her* night.

Go on, girl, get out there. Get started on your new life.

Unlike upscale Green Harbor, fifteen miles south, Yarmouth, Maine, is largely a fishing and packing town and, as such, is studded with shacks and bungalows whose occupants prefer transport like F-150s and Japanese half-tons. SUVs too, of course.

But just outside of town is a cluster of nice houses set in the woods on a hillside overlooking the bay. The cars in *these* driveways are Lexuses and Acuras mostly and the SUVs here sport leather interiors and GPS systems and not, unlike their downtown neighbors, rude bumper stickers or Jesus fish.

The neighborhood even has a name: Cedar Estates.

In his tan coveralls Joseph Bingham now walked up the driveway of one of these houses, glancing at his watch. He double-checked the address to make sure he had the right house then rang the bell.

A moment later a pretty woman in her late thirties opened the door. She was thin, her hair a little frizzy,

vornehm • Fischerei- und Verpackungs-stadt • voll von • Hütten • Bewohner • Ford Pick-ups • Halbtonner • Gruppe • protzen mit • Ledersitze • Navigations-systeme • Aufkleber • Overalls • überprüfte noch einmal

kraus

Übung 50 Im folgenden Text sind sechs sachliche Fehler versteckt. Können Sie sie finden?

Yarmouth was luxurious in comparison to Green Harbor. People in Yarmouth preferred driving big sport utility vehicles and pickup trucks with flower stickers on them. Houses in Green Harbor overlooked the bay but were quite run down. Joseph Bingham was wearing a tan suit when he walked up the driveway of one of the houses of Cedar Estates. He made a phone call to make sure he was at the right address. Then he rang the bell and the door was opened by a woman with very straight hair.

Without Jonathan **93**

and even through the screen door she smelled of alcohol. She wore skintight jeans and a white sweater.

'Yeah?'

'I'm with the cable company.' He showed her the ID. 'I have to reset your converter boxes.'

She blinked. 'The TV?'

'That's right.'

'They were working yesterday.' She turned to look hazily at the gray glossy rectangle of the large set in her living room. 'Wait, I was watching CNN earlier. It was fine.'

'You're only getting half the channels you're supposed to. The whole neighborhood is. We have to reset them manually. Or I can reschedule if –'

'Naw, it's okay. Don't wanta miss *COPS*. Come on in.'

Joseph walked inside, felt her eyes on him. He got this a lot. His career wasn't the best in the world and he wasn't classically good-looking but he was in great shape – he worked out every day – and he'd been told he 'exuded' some kind of masculine energy. He didn't know about that. He liked to think he just had a lot of self-confidence.

'You want a drink?' she asked.

hauteng

wie durch einen Schleier • glänzend • Rechteck

einen anderen Termin machen

trainierte • ströme ... aus

Welches Verb passt in welchen Satz? Orden Sie claimed, come back, realize, seemed, supposed zu.

Übung 51

1. Joseph Bingham _____ he worked for a cable company.

2. He offered to _____ another time.

3. The woman didn't _____ that her converter boxes had to be reset.

4. Joseph told her she was _____ to get more channels than she did at the moment.

5. Going by the smell she _____ to have been drinking quite a lot of alcohol.

Without Jonathan

'Can't on the job.'

'Sure?'

'Yep.'

Joseph in fact wouldn't have minded a drink. But this wasn't the place for it. Besides he was looking forward to a nice glass of spicy Pinot Noir after he finished here. It often surprised people that somebody in his line of work liked – and knew about – wines.

würzig

'I'm Barbara.'

'Hi, Barbara.'

She led him through the house to each of the cable boxes, sipping her drink as she went. She was drinking straight bourbon, it seemed.

pur

'You have kids,' Joseph said, nodding at the picture of two young children on a table in the den. 'They're great, aren't they?'

'If you like pests,' she muttered.

Nervensägen

He clicked buttons on the cable box and stood up. 'Any others?'

'Last box's in the bedroom. Upstairs. I'll show you. Wait …' She went off and refilled her glass. Then joined him again. Barbara led him up the stairs and paused at the top of the landing. Again, she looked him over.

oben am
Treppenabsatz

Übung 52   Entscheiden Sie sich für die richtige Zukunftsform und kreuzen Sie sie an.

1. Joseph _____ have a drink after finishing this job.

  was about to   was going to   will

2. Barbara said: 'I _____ upstairs and show you the cable box.'

  am going   will be going   will go

'Where are your kids tonight?' he asked.

'The pests're at the bastard's,' she said, laughing sourly at her own joke. 'We're doing the joint custody thing, my ex and me.' — gemeinsames Sorgerecht

'So you're all alone here in this big house?'

'Yeah. Pity, huh?' — schade

Joseph didn't know if it was or not. She definitely didn't seem pitiful. — mitleiderregend

'So,' he said, 'Which room's the box in?' They'd stalled in the hallway. — stehen geblieben

'Yeah. Sure. Follow me,' she said, her voice low and seductive.

In the bedroom she sat on the unmade bed and sipped the drink. He found the cable box and pushed the on-button of the set. — Fernseher • ging

It crackled to life. CNN was on. — knisternd an •

'Could you try the remote,' he said, looking around the room. — Fernbedienung

'Sure,' Barbara said groggily. She turned away and as soon as she did, Joseph came up behind her with the rope that he'd just taken from his pocket. He slipped it around her neck and twisted it tight, using a pencil for leverage. A brief scream was stifled as her throat — benommen — Hebelkraft • — erstickt

3. Barbara told Joseph that the kids _____ with their father tonight.

    would have stayed   would be staying   will be staying

4. Joseph said that by tomorrow Barbara _____ receive more channels.

    was going to   will   would be able to

5. Joseph thought to himself:

'If I'm fast enough Barbara _____.'

    won't fight   won't be fighting   wouldn't be fighting

96 Without Jonathan

closed up and she tried desperately to escape, to turn, to scratch him with her nails. The liquor soaked the bedspread as the glass fell to the carpet and rolled against the wall.

In a few minutes she was dead.

Joseph sat beside the body, catching his breath. Barbara had fought surprisingly hard. It had taken all his strength to keep her pinned down and let the garrotte do its job.

He pulled on latex gloves and wiped away whatever prints he'd left in the room. Then he dragged Barbara's body off the bed and into the center of the room. He pulled her sweater off, undid the button of her jeans.

But then he paused. Wait. What was his name supposed to be?

Frowning, he thought back to his conversation last night.

What'd he called himself?

Then he nodded. That's right. He'd told Marissa Cooper his name was Dale O'Banion. A glance at the clock. Not even seven P.M. Plenty of time to finish up here and get to Green Harbor, where she was waiting and they had a decent Pinot Noir by the glass.

Marginal glossary:
Alkohol • Tagesdecke

sie auf dem Boden niederzuhalten • Garrotte (Würgeisen)

knöpfte ... auf

anständig • Glas Pinot Noir

Übung 53   Wen beschreiben die folgenden Adjektive – Marissa, Joseph alias Dale, Barbara oder Jonathan? Ordnen Sie den Wörtern die richtigen Namen zu.

1. selfish
2. drunk
3. lonely
4. cold-blooded
5. crazy about boats
6. optimistic

Without Jonathan **97**

He unzipped Barbara's jeans then started tugging them down to her ankles.

öffnete den Reißverschluss von • zog sie ... herunter • Knöchel • menschenleer

Marissa Cooper sat on a bench in a small, deserted park, huddled against the cold wind that swept over the Green Harbor wharf.

Through the evergreens swaying in the breeze she was watching the couple lounging in the enclosed stern of the large boat tied up to the dock nearby.
Like so many boat names this one was a pun: *Maine Street.*
She'd finished her shopping, buying some fun lingerie (wondering, a little discouraged, if anyone else would ever see her wearing it) and had been on her way to the restaurant when the lights of the harbor – and the gently rocking motion of this elegant boat – caught her attention.
Through the plastic windows on the rear deck of the *Maine Street,* she saw the couple sipping champagne and sitting close together, a handsome pair – he was tall and in very good shape, plenty of salt-and-pepper hair, and she, blonde and pretty. They were laughing

Nadelbäume • die sich ... wogen • das es sich bequem gemacht hatte • Heck • Wortspiel • verrückt

grau meliert

Auf welche Wörter oder Wendungen im Text beziehen sich die folgenden Beschreibungen?

Übung 54

1. to pull down
2. gray hair
3. to open something
4. empty
6. good-looking couple
7. physically fit
8. a word or phrase that sounds like another word

98 Without Jonathan

wurde zuge-
knallt

and talking. Flirting like crazy. Then, finishing their champagne, they disappeared down into the cabin. The teak door slammed shut.

Frösteln • über-
fiel •
mutig •
alle Achtung •
schweifen •
beruflich
machen

Thinking about the lingerie in the bag she carried, thinking about resuming dating, Marissa again pictured Dale O'Banion. Wondered how this evening would go. A chill hit her and she rose and went on to the restaurant.

Sipping a glass of fine Chardonnay (sitting boldly at the bar by herself – way to go, girl!), Marissa let her thoughts shift to what she might do for work. She wasn't in a huge hurry. There was the insurance money. The savings accounts too. The house was nearly paid for. But it wasn't that she needed to work. It was that she wanted to. Teaching. Or writing. Maybe she could get a job for one of the local newspapers.

Or she might even go to medical school. She remembered the times Jonathan would tell her about some of the things he was doing at the hospital and she'd understood them perfectly. Marissa had a very logical mind and had been a brilliant student. If she'd gone on to graduate school* years ago, she could've gotten a full scholarship for her master's degree.

Vollstipendium

---

info

Das amerikanische Universitätssystem ist anders aufgebaut und stärker strukturiert als das deutsche. Es besteht zum Beispiel Anwesenheitspflicht. An den privaten oder staatlichen Colleges, die entweder eigenständig oder Teil einer Universität sind, kann man ein vierjähriges undergraduate-Studium absolvieren, mit dem Bachelor-Abschluss abgehen und sich dann eine Arbeit suchen. Wer weitermachen will, kann sich um einen Studienplatz an der Graduate School, einer Universität, bewerben und einen Master- oder Doktortitel erwerben.

Without Jonathan 99

More wine.

Feeling sad then feeling exhilarated. Her moods bobbed like orange buoys marking the lobster traps sitting on the floor of the gray ocean.

euphorisch • schwankten hin und her • Bojen • Hummerfallen

The deadly ocean.

She thought again about the man she was waiting for in this romantic, candlelit restaurant.

mit Kerzen beleuchtet

A moment of panic. Should she call Dale and tell him that she just wasn't ready for this yet?

Go home, have another wine, put on some Mozart, light a fire. Be content with your own company.

She began to lift her hand to signal the bartender for the check.

But suddenly a memory came to her. A memory from life *before* Jonathan. She remembered being a little girl, riding a pony beside her grandfather, who sat on his tall Appaloosa. She recalled watching the lean old man calmly draw a revolver and sight down on a rattlesnake that was coiled to strike at Marissa's Shetland. The sudden shot blew the snake into a bloody mess on the sand.

hager • auf ... richtete • sich zusammengeringelt hatte • blutige Masse

He'd worried that the girl would be upset, having witnessed the death. Up the trail, they'd dismounted.

abgestiegen

Welche Antwort stimmt?
Tragen Sie ein T für true oder ein F für false in die Kästchen ein.

Übung 55

1. How does Marissa feel?
completely depressed   up and down   happy

2. Why did Marissa's grandfather shoot at the snake?
to teach his granddaughter how to shoot
the snake was going to bite Marissa's horse   to show off

3. Was Marissa looking forward to meeting Dale?
not at all   a little   she wasn't sure

He'd crouched beside her and told her not to feel bad – that he'd *had* to shoot the snake 'But it's all right, honey. His soul's on its way to heaven.'

She'd frowned.

'What's the matter?' her grandfather had asked.

'That's too bad. I want him to go to hell.'

Marissa missed that tough little girl. And she knew that if she called Dale to cancel, she would have failed. It would be like letting the snake bite her pony.

No, Dale was the first step, an absolutely necessary step, to getting on with her life without Jonathan.

And then there he was – a good-looking, balding man. Great body too, she observed, in a dark suit. Beneath it he wore a black T-shirt, not a white polyester shirt and stodgy tie you saw so often in this area.

She waved and he responded with a charming smile.

He walked up to her. 'Marissa? I'm Dale.'

A firm grip.

She gave him back one equally firm.

He sat next to her at the bar and ordered a glass of Pinot Noir. Sniffed it with pleasure then clinked his glass to hers.

They sipped.

um abzusagen

nichtssagend

Händedruck

schnupperte •
stieß ... mit ihr
an

Übung 56   Die folgenden Wörter sind das Gegenteil von Wörtern im Text auf dieser Seite. Können Sie sie finden?

1. to succeed

2. rarely

3. ugly

4. to confirm

5. to walk away from someone

6. disgust

7. unnecessary

Without Jonathan **101**

'I wasn't sure if you'd be late,' she said. 'Sometimes it's hard to get off work when you want to.'

Another sniff of wine. 'I pretty much control my own hours,' he said.

They chatted for a few minutes and then went to the hostess's stand*. The woman showed them to the table he'd reserved. A moment later they were seated next to the window. Spotlights on the outside of the restaurant shone down into the gray water; the sight troubled her at first, thinking about Jonathan in the deadly ocean, she forced her thoughts away and concentrated on Dale.

Scheinwerfer •
Anblick

They made small talk. He was divorced and had no children, though he'd always wanted them. She and Jonathan hadn't had children either, she explained. Talking about the weather in Maine, about politics.

'Been shopping?' he asked, smiling. Nodding at the pink-and-white-striped bag she'd set beside her chair.

'Long underwear,' she joked. 'It's supposed to be a cold winter.'

They talked some more, finishing one bottle of wine, then had one more glass each, though it seemed to her that she drank more than he did.

tranken ... aus

In den USA wird Service besonders großgeschrieben. In Bistros und Restaurants, auch in vielen Pizzaketten, werden die Gäste an einem Pult (stand) am Eingang von einer hostess oder einem host freundlich begrüßt, gefragt, für wie viele Personen sie einen Tisch brauchen, und dann entweder gleich hingeführt oder gebeten zu warten, bis abgeräumt und neu gedeckt ist. Danach wird man der Kellnerin oder dem Kellner vorgestellt, der oder die die weitere persönliche Betreuung übernimmt.

info

Without Jonathan

wurde langsam beschwipst •	She was getting tipsy. Watch out there, girl. Keep your wits about you.
Behalte einen klaren Kopf.	But then she thought about Jonathan and drank down the glass.
	Near ten P.M. he looked around the emptying restaurant. He fixed her with his eyes and said, 'How about we go outside?'
zögerte	Marissa hesitated. Okay, this is it, she thought to herself.
	You can leave, or you can go out there with him.
Vorsatz	She thought of her resolution, she thought of Jonathan. She said, 'Yes. Let's go.'
	Outside, they walked side by side back to the deserted park she'd sat in earlier.
	They came to the same bench and she nodded at it and they sat down. Dale close beside her.
	She felt his presence – the nearness of a strong man, which she hadn't felt for some time now. And it was
erregend • beruhigend • beunruhigend	thrilling, comforting and unsettling all at the same time.
	They looked at the boat, the *Maine Street*, just visible through the trees.

Übung 57   Verbinden Sie die folgenden Sätze. Entscheiden Sie sich für eines der Bindewörter after, and, because, before, but, when, where.

1. She was getting tipsy _____ she had been drinking but had forgotten to eat something.
2. _____ Dale saw that the restaurant was getting empty he suggested going outside.
3. They sat down on a bench _____ she had been sitting earlier that evening.
4. It was thrilling and comforting sitting next to Dale _____ also unsettling.

Without Jonathan   103

They sat in silence for a few minutes, huddling against the cold.

zusammenge-
kauert

Dale stretched. His arm went along the back of the bench, not quite around her shoulders but she felt his muscles.

How strong he was, she reflected.

It was then that she glanced down and saw a twisted length of white rope protruding from his pocket, about to fall out.

verdrehtes Stück
• aus ... hängen

She nodded at it. 'You're going to lose something.'

He glanced down. Picked it up, flexed the rope in his fingers. Unwound it.

bog •
entwirrte

She wondered what it was for.

'Tool of the trade,' he said, looking at her querying frown.

Arbeitsmaterial

Then he slipped it back into his pocket.

Dale looked back to the *Maine Street*, just visible through the trees, at the couple now out of the bedroom and sipping champagne again on the rear deck.

Achterdeck

'That's him in there, the handsome guy?' he asked.

'Yes,' Marissa said, 'that's my husband. That's Jonathan.' She shivered again from the cold – and

---

5. They sat on the bench without talking _____ were huddling against the cold.

6. _____ picking up the rope he flexed and unwound it.

7. Dale watched the couple on the boat for a while _____ asking Marissa if the man was Jonathan.

104 Without Jonathan

zierlich

the disgust – as she watched him kiss the petite blonde.

She started to ask Dale if he was going to do it tonight – to murder her husband – but then decided that he, probably like most professional killers, would prefer to speak in euphemisms. She asked simply, 'When's it going to happen?'

They were now walking slowly away from the wharf; he'd seen what he needed to.

'When?' Dale asked. 'Depends. That woman in there with him? Who's she?'

Krankenschwes-ter-Schlampen

'One of his little slut nurses. I don't know. Karen, maybe.'

'She's spending the night?'

wirft sie ... raus

• klammernd

'No. I've been spying on him for a month. He'll kick her out about midnight. He can't stand clinging mistresses. There'll be another one tomorrow. But not before noon.'

Dale nodded. 'Then I'll do it tonight. After she leaves.' He glanced at Marissa. 'I'll handle it like I was telling you – after he's asleep I'll get on board, tie him up and take the boat out a few miles. Then I'll make it look

---

Übung 58   Sind die folgenden Aussagen wahr oder falsch?
Tragen Sie ein T für true oder ein F für false in die Kästchen ein.

1. Marissa had hired Dale to kill her husband and his lover.
2. Dale was going to kill Marissa's husband after his lover had left the boat.
3. Dale was very discreet and avoided talking openly about his job.
4. Marissa had been watching her husband for a long time and knew for sure that he was cheating on her with one particular single woman.

like he got tangled in the anchor line and went over- | hätte er sich
board. Has he been drinking much?' | verfangen • An-
'Is there water in the ocean?' she asked wryly. | kertau • ironisch
'Good, that'll help. Then I'll drive the boat close to
Huntington and take a raft back in. Just let her drift.' | Floß
Nodding at the *Maine Street*.
'You always make it look like an accident?' Marissa
asked, wondering if a question like this was breaking
some kind of hit-man protocol. | Killer-Spielre-
'As often as I can. That job I did tonight I mentioned? | geln
It was taking care of a woman in Yarmouth. She'd
been abusing her own kids. I mean, beating them. | missbraucht
'Pests,' she called them. Disgusting. She wouldn't stop
but the husband couldn't get the children to say any-
thing to the police, they didn't want to get her in
trouble.'
'God, how terrible.'
Dale nodded. 'I'll say. So the husband hired me. I made
it look like that rapist from Upper Falls broke in and | Vergewaltiger
killed her.'
Marissa considered this. Then she asked, 'Did you …? I
mean, you were pretending to be a rapist …' | taten so als ob
'Oh, God, no,' Dale said, frowning. 'I'd never do that. I

5. The fact that Jonathan usually consumed a fair
amount of alcohol made it easier for Dale to make the
murder look like an accident.

6. Dale told Marissa about the woman he had murdered
the day before.

7. Barbara's children lived with their father and only saw
their mother one weekend a month.

8. Marissa felt sorry for Barbara's children.

just made it *look* like I did. Believe me, it was pretty gross finding a used condom from behind that massage parlor on Knightsbridge Street.'

ekelhaft • Massagesalon

So hit men have standards, she reflected. At least some of them do.

She looked him over. 'Aren't you worried I'm a policewoman or anything? Trying to set you up. I mean, I just got your name out of that magazine. *Worldwide Soldier.*'

Ihnen etwas anzuhängen

'You do this long enough, you get a feel for who're real customers and who aren't. Anyway, I spent the last week checking you out. You're legitimate.'

in Ordnung

If a woman paying someone twenty-five thousand dollars to kill her husband can be called legitimate.

Speaking of which …

She took a thick envelope out of her pocket. Handed it to Dale. It disappeared into the pocket with the white rope.

'Dale … wait, you're name's not really Dale, is it?'

'No, but it's the one I'm using for this job.'

'Okay, well, Dale, he won't feel anything?' she asked.

'No pain.'

Übung 59 Die folgenden Wörter haben mehrere Bedeutungen.
Zwei von drei Möglichkeiten stimmen. Welche sind es?
Kreuzen Sie sie an.

1. pretty

  ziemlich   hübsch   dumm

2. current

  Währung   Strömung   aktuell

3. picture

  sich vorstellen   Bild   Krug

Without Jonathan

'Not a thing. Even if he were conscious that water's so cold he'll probably pass out and die of shock before he drowns.'

in Ohnmacht fallen

They'd reached the end of the park. Dale asked, 'You're sure about doing this?'

And Marissa asked herself, 'Am I sure about wanting Jonathan dead?'

Jonathan – the man who tells me he goes fishing with the boys every weekend but in truth takes his nurses out on the boat for his little trysts. Who spends our savings on them. Who announced a few years after getting married that he'd had a vasectomy and didn't want the children he'd promised we'd have. Who speaks to me like a ten-year-old about his job or current events, never even hearing me say, 'I understand, honey. I'm a smart woman.' Who nagged me into quitting a job I loved. Who flies into a rage every time I want to go back to work. Who complains whenever I wear sexy clothes in public but who stopped sleeping with me years ago. Who gets violent whenever I bring up divorce because a doctor at a teaching hospital needs a wife to get ahead … and because he's a control freak.

Schäferstünd-chen • Sterilisation

aktuell • mir die Hölle heiß gemacht hat, bis • einen Wutan-fall bekommt

Lehrkranken-haus • um Kar-riere zu machen

4. book

reservieren	backen	Buch

5. trunk

Rüssel	Kofferraum	Getränk

6. table

Tabelle	Tisch	Etikett

7. kind

Kind	Art	freundlich

8. boot

Computer hochfahren	Boot	Stiefel

108 Without Jonathan

Marissa Cooper suddenly pictured the shattered corpse
Fleck of a rattlesnake lying bloody on a hot patch of yellow
Texas sand so many years ago.
That's too bad. I want him to go to hell …
'I'm sure,' she said.
Dale shook her hand and said, 'I'll take care of things
from here. Go home. You should practice playing the
trauernd grieving widow.'
'I can handle that,' Marissa said, 'I've been a grieving
wife for years.'
Pulling her coat collar up high, she returned to the
parking lot, not looking back at either her husband or
at the man who was about to kill him. She climbed
ließ den Motor into her Toyota and fired up the engine, found some
an rock and roll on the radio, turned the volume up high
and left Green Harbor.
kurbelte … her- Marissa cranked the windows down, filling the car
unter • kühl • with sharp autumn air, rich with the scent of wood
Geruch smoke and old leaves and drove fast through the night,
thinking about her future, about her life without
Jonathan.

Übung 60 Finden Sie die im folgenden Text versteckten vier sachlichen Fehler.

Marissa was not quite sure whether she wanted Dale to go ahead
and kill her husband. Dale told her he would make sure that
everything would work out. Jonathan had given Marissa a hard
time because she couldn't have children. Also he had cheated on
her numerous times. These and other reasons had driven Marissa to
hire Dale and to pay his fee of twenty thousand dollars. She found
Dale very attractive but realized there was no future for them.

Lösungen

1
1. Doug had suggested to Pete that he came on down solo.
   Doug had asked Pete why didn't he come on down solo.
2. He said he knew that he said that he would clean up the garage.
3. She said that no, it could keep. She thought it was a great idea.
4. Pete thought that he knew she thought it'd be a great idea.
5. She came back and said it was his father.

2
1. Mo did not want him to be on the phone.
2. I will go visit Doug then.
3. I think Saturday would be fine.
4. It is getting late.
5. He had looked around the store.
6. He had had to steal it.

3
1. He strolled calmly out of the store.
2. She was going out with another man.
3. He crept up and pushed him over a cliff.
4. Pete didn't know anything about crimes.
5. Hank grabbed on to a tree root but he lost his hold.
6. None of the criminals in those shows seemed very clever.

4
1. If Roy had not forgotten to look for witnesses he wouldn't have got caught.
   oder If Roy had forgotten to look for witnesses he would have got caught.
2. If he hadn't read it cover to cover he wouldn't have seen how Roy had planned the crime.
   oder If he had read it cover to cover he would have seen how Roy had planned the crime.
3. If he hadn't made sure he got away with the crime he would have gone to jail for life.

5
1. 'Triangle' became Pete's bible.
2. He read the book from cover to cover.
3. He wanted to make sure he got away with the crime.
4. She changed the subject.
5. 'Oh Doug?' she said, sounding irritated.
6. Mo was starting to spend a lot of time online.

Lösungen

6   **1.** F Doug schien wirklich Interesse an Pete zu haben.
    2. T Mo hatte Doug erzählt, dass Pete sich für Computer und Sport interessierte.
    3. F Pete genoss es, mit Mo und Doug zu Abend zu essen.
    4. F Pete fand durch einen Brief in Mos Handtasche heraus, dass Doug und Mo eine Beziehung hatten.
    5. T Pete plante, Doug umzubringen.
    6. F Pete kam auf den Mordplan, nachdem er einen Film gesehen hatte.
    7. T Mo hoffte, dass sich Pete und Doug verstehen würden.
    8. T Mo und Pete verbrachten viel Zeit zusammen, bevor Mo Doug kennenlernte.
    9. T Das Leben war für Pete total anders gewesen, bevor Mo Doug kennenlernte.
   10. T Mo veränderte sich sehr, nachdem sie Doug kennenlernte.
   11. F Mo und Pete planten eine gemeinsame Reise.
   12. T Mo würde Doug am Sonntagnachmittag treffen.

7   **1.** The clerk at the motel said that he was going to connect Pete.
    2. Before someone had answered the telephone Pete had hung up.
    3. While Mo and Doug were talking inside the motel room Pete was listening outside to their conversation.
    4. Doug told Mo he wanted her to paint her nails bright red.
    5. Recently Mo had been painting her nails peach.

8   **1.** Pete was upset when he heard what Mo said.
    2. Pete kept quiet while he was listening to Mo and Doug talking.
    3. Mo was worried that Pete might find out about her affair.
    4. Mo was used to a certain lifestyle.
    5. Doug was being sarcastic when he was talking about doing something with Pete.

9   **1.** Doug got to know Pete.
    2. It had felt like he was the boss.
    3. Pete and Doug went to a ball game together.
    4. They saw him on the weekend.
    5. Doug and Pete hung out together.
    6. Pete was only smart when it came to computers and sports.
    7. Pete had wrung his hands together.
    8. Doug kept his hands off Mo.
    9. It had taken all his willpower not to scream.
   10. He shook with fury.
   11. He had thrown himself on the couch.
   12. Mo had driven Pete to the airport.
   13. Pete fell asleep.
   14. He had gone to the bookstore.
   15. He had stolen a copy of 'Triangle'.

112   Lösungen

10   **1.** Roy was in an **unusually** good mood.
     2. Pete gave Mo a really **hard** hug.
     3. Mo thought that Pete **genuinely** loved her.
     4. He could **easily** see through Mo.
     5. Pete was acting very **well**.
     6. He had noticed that women would often stand **close** to him.
     7. He made **sure** he read all the important passages in the book.
     8. He knew he had to plan very **carefully**.
     9. Pete was **seriously** thinking about killing Doug.
   10. Hank had fallen **staight** onto his right side.
   11. He was **severely** injured.

11   **1.** How **are** you doing?
     2. **Are** you hungry?
     3. **I** sure am.
     4. **Do you** think you can handle two real men?
     5. **Do** you have a girlfriend?

12   **1.** **After** Pete had pretended to think for a minute he suggested going hiking
        somewhere.
     2. Pete suggested going hiking **because** he had read about the murder in 'Triangle'.
     3. **However** Doug suggested going hunting instead.
     4. **Although** Pete had planned to kill Doug in a hiking accident he agreed
        to go hunting.
     5. Pete pretended that he didn't know anything about guns **so that**
        Doug would not suspect anything.
     6. **While** Doug was loading the gun Pete was watching him.
     7. **As soon as** Pete saw Doug's house he realized that Mo would love
        the luxury of it.
     8. Doug didn't seem to distrust Pete **and** even invited him into his house.

13   **1.** She wanted to **see** him **off**. (= **verabschieden**)
     2. She hoped they would **hit** it **off**. (= **sich auf Anhieb verstehen**)
     3. They had **messed up** his plan. (= **ruiniert**)
     4. If Roy had **looked around** he would have seen that there were witnesses.
        (= **sich umgesehen**)
     5. Doug thought that Pete was a beginner but it **turned out** that Pete
        was a good shot. (= **stellte sich heraus**)
     6. 'Triangle' was such a good story Pete didn't even have to **make up** a plan
        for himself. (= **ausdenken**)
     7. He was afraid his plan wouldn't **work out**. (= **klappen**)

Lösungen **113**

14
1.	lie	☒ lügen	☐ legen	☒ liegen
2.	scan	☐ erkunden	☒ scannen	☒ absuchen
3.	miss	☒ verpassen	☐ ausmisten	☒ vermissen
4.	bright	☒ hell	☐ herrlich	☒ klug
5.	sink	☒ Waschbecken	☒ untergehen	☐ singen

15 Pete was spying on Mo and Doug who were sitting in a restaurant. He couldn't see them but he listened to what they were saying. They were talking about moving in together. Mo was concerned about Pete knowing about their relationship because she didn't want him to divorce her. She was accustomed to having a certain amount of money and didn't want to give up her lifestyle. Pete nearly fainted when he heard that. Inside Doug was giggling and talked in a strange tone of voice about dealing with Pete.

16
1. In Pete's opinion Mo and Doug only thought about themselves.
2. Doug drank a whole bottle of beer by himself.
3. Mo was at home all by herself.
4. Pete thought that if Doug was gone Mo and he would be able to go hiking all by themselves.
5. Doug said to Pete: 'Help yourself to a bottle of beer.'

17
1. Doug reached out and took Pete's rifle, didn't he?
2. Pete had been planning on holding Doug's gun for him, hadn't he?
3. When Doug was at the top of the fence he was going to shoot him, wasn't he?
4. You want me to go first, don't you?
5. Then I'll hand the guns over to you, shall I?
6. Go on, will you?
7. This is it, isn't it?
8. He's going to shoot me, isn't he?
9. Last month I left the motel too early, didn't I?
10. If I run, he'll chase me down and shoot me, won't he?
11. Even if he shoots me in the back he'll just claim it's an accident, won't he?

18
1. Pete didn't trust Doug.
2. Roy probably hadn't imagined he would spend his life in prison.
3. Doug tried to shoot a squirrel.
4. Pete was first to climb the fence even though he didn't really want to.
5. Doug suggested shooting a rabbit.
6. Mo was probably thinking Pete and Doug were having a good time.
7. Roy's plan had been very close to perfect.
8. Pete tried to find a chance to shoot Doug.
9. Pete was very nervous as he thought Doug might shoot him any minute.
10. Doug had suggested going hunting.

19
1. Pete had gotten rid of **both** 'Triangle' **and** Doug. (= sowohl ... als auch)
2. Mo's fingernails were painted **neither** bright red **nor** peach. (= weder ... noch)
3. **Either** Mo was going to believe Pete was innocent **or** not. (= entweder ... oder)
4. **Both** Pete's father **and** his mother shared custody of him. (= und)
5. **Neither** the flight attendant **nor** Mo suspected Pete of knowing anything.
   (= weder ... noch)

20
1. [F] Die unerwartete Wendung der Geschichte ist, dass Pete Mos Bruder ist.
2. [T] Pete hat es geschafft, den „perfekten" Mord zu begehen.
3. [T] Pete hatte den Mord an Doug geplant, um Mo dafür zu bestrafen, dass sie seinen Vater fallen gelassen hatte.
4. [T] Pete schien der Stewardess und allen anderen, Mo eingeschlossen, leidzutun.
5. [T] Mo ist am Boden zerstört, gibt aber trotzdem nicht zu, dass Doug ihr Freund war.
6. [F] Leider hatte Pete vergessen, 'Triangle' wegzuwerfen.
7. [T] Doug wäre gerne Pete losgeworden, um Mo für sich zu haben.
8. [F] Petes Vater lebte in Colorado.
9. [F] Doug hinterließ eine Frau und zwei Töchter.
10. [T] Pete ist noch nicht einmal elf Jahre alt.

21
1. Patsy Randolph was Dr. Harry Bernstein's **patient**.
2. Patsy claimed her husband was driving her to **insanity**.
3. She was **afraid** of her husband.
4. Harry could see Patsy was **troubled**.
5. She believed her husband **intended** to drive her crazy.

22
1. Tears are important **barometers** of emotional weather.
2. Harry **studied** Patsy closely.
3. Patsy wore **impeccable** makeup.
4. Patsy told him that it had happened **a couple of** times.
5. Harry **paid close attention** to what Patsy said.
6. Patsy was **pacing** across the room.
7. She told Harry that the ghost just **rambled on and on**.
8. It was **hard to hear** what the ghost was saying.
9. The ghost was talking about **incidents** from her childhood.
10. The voice sounded **sort of** like her husband's voice.
11. Patsy didn't **respond** for a minute.
12. Harry **continued to take his notes**.
13. Patsy admitted it sounded **ridiculous**.

23
1. proud (stolz) – Patsy
2. good-looking (gut aussehend) – Peter
3. professional (professionell) – Harry
4. upset (durcheinander) – Patsy
5. compulsive (zwanghaft) – Patsy
6. concerned (besorgt) – Harry

Lösungen **115**

24 **1.** Patsy told Harry that Sally **had said** that maybe Peter **was** jealous of **her**.
2. Patsy said that **she** just **didn't know** why Peter **was doing** it.
3. Harry asked Patsy whether **she had talked** to him about this.
4. Patsy said that the ceramic birds **were** made by Boehm. She asked Harry
if he **knew** about the company.
5. Patsy told Harry that when **their** father **had died** Steve and **her had split** the
inheritance but that he **had got** most of the family heirlooms.
6. Patsy told Harry that when **she was** twelve **she had broken** one of the birds.
She had run inside as **she had been very excited** about something and **had
wanted** to tell **her** father about it.
7. Harry asked Patsy what **had happened** yesterday.
8. Patsy told Harry that the morning after Peter **had started** whispering to **her
she had found** one of the birds broken.
9. Harry asked Patsy what exactly **she had heard**.

25 **1.** F Harrys Sitzungen mit seinen Patienten dauerten immer länger als geplant.
T **Harry sorgte dafür, dass seine Sitzungen nie länger dauerten,
als sie sollten.**
F Harry stimmte seine Sitzungen zeitlich auf die Bedürfnisse
seiner Patienten ab.

2. F Patsy sah immer perfekt aus.
F Patsys Make-up war verschmiert und ihre Kleidung war durcheinander.
T **Abgesehen von ihrem Make-up sah Patsy sehr unordentlich aus.**

3. F Harry fühlte sich nicht in der Lage, Patsy zu helfen.
F Harry war über die heutige Sitzung frustriert.
T **Harry glaubte, dass die heutige Sitzung sehr wichtig gewesen war.**

4. F Miriam war wütend, dass ihr Chef sich wie ein Kind verhielt.
F Miriam war es gewöhnt, dass Harry laut lachte.
T **Miriam war überrascht über Harrys Benehmen.**

26 **1.** **Marrying** seemed to be the right thing to do for Harry and Linda.
2. After the wedding he would be **starting** his internship.
3. Linda was quickly **beginning** to change Harry's life.
4. Harry's life was **heading** in the wrong direction.
5. He was **hanging** up his sign outside his office.
6. Harry was always **worrying** about the high bills.

27 **1.** Harry was very **bad** at what he did.
2. His patients **didn't like**/**hated** him and so they **never returned**.
3. **Everybody understands** me, sure **we haven't got any money**,
money **is** everything.
4. Their troubles were **always very serious**.
5. He **did** what he really wanted to do.

28
1. A lot of patients **whined about** minor problems.
2. He'd never **bothered** to read all the journals.
3. He found Internet sites **devoted to** psychotic behaviour.
4. He was **rereading** an article in the 'Journal of Psychoses' which he'd been **thrilled** to find.
5. He **glanced** out of the window and **realized** that it wasn't the kettle at all.
6. Patsy's clothes weren't **pressed**.
7. Her hair hadn't been **shampooed** for days.
8. Patsy sounded **timid**.
9. Harry suggested **postponing** their usual work.
10. Harry wanted to deal with the crisis **face-to-face**.
11. Patsy sat in the armchair **across from** his desk.

29
1. **What** was Patsy's husband doing?/
   What was Patsy's husband whispering to her?
2. **Who** was it and **who** was he pretending to be?
3. **What** did Patsy think?/**Whose** timbre did Patsy think it was?
4. **What** did Patsy study?/**What** did Patsy do?
5. **Where** had Peter gone?/**What** had Peter gone out for?
6. **What** did Patsy do?/**What** did Patsy clear?
7. **What** did Patsy do with her purse?/**How** did Patsy click the purse latch?
8. **How** long did Harry wait?
9. **What** did Harry ask Patsy to do/assume?
10. **What** was the most difficult part of being a therapist?

30
1. Harry suggested that Patsy **projected her own thoughts onto what she heard**.
   - [X] **Er gab zu bedenken, dass Patsy sich einbildete, was sie hörte.**
   - [ ] Er gab zu bedenken, dass Patsy sich selbst sprechen hörte.
   - [ ] Er gab zu bedenken, dass Patsy einfach träumte.

2. Patsy was like a student **who'd been given a gold star** by a teacher.
   - [ ] Sie benahm sich wie eine Schülerin, die einen Goldbarren bekommen hatte.
   - [ ] Sie benahm sich wie eine Schülerin, die eine gute Note bekommen hatte.
   - [X] **Sie benahm sich wie eine Schülerin, die eine Auszeichnung bekommen hatte.**

3. Patsy asked Harry whether he would have to **charge her double**.
   - [ ] Patsy fragte Harry, ob er besonders wütend auf sie sein würde.
   - [X] **Patsy wollte wissen, ob Harry das Doppelte seines regulären Satzes verlangen würde.**
   - [ ] Patsy wollte wissen, ob sie für zwei Stunden bezahlen müsste.

31
1. Her heart was thudding **harder** than ever before.
2. Patsy was **more hysterical** than he had imagined she would be.
3. The Randolph's apartment building was **further** away than Harry thought.
4. Patsy Randolph was among the **wealthiest** clients Harry had.
5. It might be one of the **most luxurious** high-rises in the area.

6. Harry was aware that a therapist's contact with his patients had to be handled **more carefully** than with other people.

7. Peter Randolph might well be the **trimmest** and **most athletic** man Harry had ever seen.

8. Peter Randolph was **angrier** than Harry had imagined and also **more bewildered** than Harry had ever seen a man.

9. You couldn't find **more supple** leather slippers in all New York.

32 1. Patsy's hair was **dirty**.
2. Her makeup looked **okay**.
3. The lobby had no **carpet**.
4. Peter had called for **help**.
5. The ghosts told Patsy to **leave**.

33 1. AC ☒ **air conditioning = Klimaanlage**   ☐ aircraft
2. ID ☐ independent driver   ☒ **identity card = Personalausweis**
3. PC ☒ **politically correct = politisch korrekt**   ☐ police car
4. TV ☐ televised   ☒ **television = Fernsehen**
5. ER ☒ **emergency room = Notaufnahme**   ☐ Elvis Revival

34 1. If Patsy **claimed** that Peter was trying to drive her crazy the judge wouldn't believe her.
2. Who knows what **would happen** if Patsy was hospitalized.
3. Everything would be perfect if Patsy **stayed** in control.
4. Patsy **would have known** why Harry wanted to see her husband if she had been honest to herself.
5. If Patsy **had seemed** like a nut case to the cop why had he not taken her to a hospital?

35 1. What are Peter's feelings for his wife?
Ⓣ **Er liebt sie sehr.**   Ⓕ Er hasst sie.   Ⓕ Sie ist ihm gleichgültig.

2. When did Patsy start feeling bad?
Ⓕ vor einem halben Jahr   Ⓣ **vor ein paar Monaten**   Ⓕ vor einer Woche

3. Does Harry think he can help Patsy?
Ⓕ nein   Ⓣ **ja**   Ⓕ vielleicht

4. How does Patsy feel towards her father?
Ⓕ Sie mag ihn nicht.   Ⓣ **Sie ist wütend auf ihn.**   Ⓕ Sie vermisst ihn.

5. Peter thinks he knows why Patsy is upset.
Ⓕ Sie glaubt, dass Peter ausziehen will.   Ⓕ Sie glaubt, dass Peter sich von ihr scheiden lassen will.   Ⓣ **Sie glaubt, dass Peter sie betrügt.**

118   **Lösungen**

36 Harry asked Patsy's **brother** about her financial situation. First Peter got angry
at Harry but eventually he calmed down and explained about the agreement
he and Patsy had before they got married. If **Penelope** (Patsy was just a nickname)
didn't love him anymore he would get all the money. Harry apologized
to Peter and explained to him that he needed his help. However Peter **refused.**
He was jealous of Harry.

37 **1.** Harry thinks that patients need a **strong** hand.
2. Harry tells Peter not to **spoil** Patsy.
3. Harry was a very **passionate** psychiatrist.
4. One of his professor's expressions had been that you have to kill or to **heal.**
5. Patsy came to see Harry without having **arranged** an appointment.

38 **1.** Harry expected **of** his patients that they made an appointment with his receptionist.
2. He could see that Patsy was very upset **about** something.
3. Harry could tell that Patsy's fingernails hadn't been cleaned **in** ages.
4. Normally Harry avoided physical contact with his patients but **during** this session
he felt it was okay to sit next to Pasty.
5. Patsy wanted Harry to admit her **to** hospital but he refused.
6. Harry asked Patsy to repeat **after** him that she was just imagining things.

39 **1.** Patsy kept saying that there was no ghost and that her father was dead **and she**
found she was calming each time.
2. Harry told Patsy **to take the last bird and smash the hell out of it.**
3. Harry told Patsy: **'You bet you can. Just give permission to'.**
4. Harry thought **'the hell with transference'.**
5. Peter told Patsy that **they were supposed to go to Jack and Louise's**
that night.
6. Patsy replied that **she didn't feel like.**
7. However he told her **she wasn't getting out of it.**
8. In the end Patsy said that she had **to take care of** a few things first.

40 **1.** ☐F Patsy war schlechter Laune, als sie sich ein Glas Wein eingoss.
2. ☐T **Peter Randolph war nicht bewusst, dass seine Frau ihn umbringen**
würde.
3. ☐T **Patsy hörte nicht auf, auf Peter mit dem Hammer einzuschlagen, bis**
er tot war.
4. ☐F Sie zitterte am ganzen Körper, als sie einen Tagebucheintrag über die
Ereignisse machte.
5. ☐F Die Nachbarn hörten sie weinen und riefen einen Notfallwagen, weil sie um
sie besorgt waren.
6. ☐T **Harry hatte Patsy zum letzten Mal gesehen, als er ihr gesagt hatte,**
dass sie den letzten Vogel mit einem Hammer zertrümmern sollte.
7. ☐T **Patsys Anwalt sah perfekt aus, während Harry schlimm aussah.**

Lösungen

41 **1.** Patsy's lawyer couldn't help *thinking* that something was wrong with Harry.
2. He suggested *meeting* Harry to discuss how they were going to handle Patsy's case.
3. He hoped *to find* a way to help Patsy.
4. Patsy obviously wanted to avoid *spending* the rest of her life in jail.
5. The lawyer offered *to help out* Harry with a few thousand dollars.
6. When Harry went into Patsy's room she didn't seem *to recognize* him.
7. She used to like *talking* to Harry during their sessions.
8. When Patsy started *talking/to talk* about ghosts Harry got slightly impatient.

42 **1.** How does Patsy feel?
F unglücklich   T ängstlich   F verwirrt

2. What was the article about that Harry had found?
F Halluzinationen   F Unzurechnungsfähigkeit   T Diagnose

3. Where was Patsy?
F in einer   T in einem Gefängnis-   F in der psychiatrischen
Gefängniszelle   krankenhaus   Abteilung eines Gefängnisses

43 Harry didn't believe what Patsy ~~were~~ *was* telling him. On the contrary he thought she was a ~~well~~ *good* actress and was actually trying to deceive ~~himself~~ *him*. However Patsy kept talking about ~~ghost~~ *ghosts* and how she was afraid of them. She told Harry people ~~wants~~ *wanted* to kill her. She finally stopped when Harry told her in detail about the article he had ~~founded~~ *found* and how he believed she was making it all up.

44 **1.** The clothes *that* Patsy was wearing were torn and dirty.
2. The ghosts *that* Patsy kept mentioning didn't exist.
3. People *whose* minds are disturbed don't make jokes.
4. The literature *that* Harry had read dealt with psychotics.
5. Patients *who* are genuine mental health cases don't wear perfect makeup.
6. Patsy's father *whom* she resented very much had just been used as part of her story.

45 **1.** Patsy admitted to Harry it *had been* her goal to kill her husband.
2. She was shocked though that he *had known* about it all the time.
3. Before visiting Patsy Harry *wrote* a bill that he was going to give to her.
4. He *left* her a million dollars so she would be able to pay her lawyer.
5. Harry warned Patsy that if she *made* a complaint about the food they would put her on a tube.
6. First Patsy pretended she *had* not *done* anything wrong.

46 **1.** In which part of the USA does Marissa Cooper live?
F an der Westküste   T an der Ostküste
2. What had Marissa and Jonathan celebrated last May?
F ihre Geburtstage   T ihren Hochzeitstag
3. Where had they driven to a thousand times?
T zum Einkaufszentrum   F ins Stadtzentrum

120   Lösungen

47 **1.** In dieser Gegend schienen alle verrückt auf Boote zu sein.
   In this part of coastal Maine you couldn't avoid boats.
2. Marissas Herz machte einen kleinen Satz, als sie eine Anzeige im Schaufenster
   des Geschäfts sah.
   Her heart did a little thud at what she saw.
3. Wie am Ende jeden Tages trabten die Kühe eine hinter der anderen zurück zur
   Scheune.
   … cows, walking single file in their spontaneous day-end commute back
   to the barn.
4. Marissa war ziemlich bestürzt, dass das Boot in der Anzeige genauso aussah wie
   Jonathans Boot.
   But what had struck her hard was that the boat pictured in the ad …
   was a Chris-Craft. Just like Jonathan's boat.
5. Jonathan ging fischen, als ob es sein Job wäre, und er brachte immer nach
   Hause, was er gefangen hatte.
   … fishing like an old cod dockhand. Her husband would bring home to
   Marissa the best of his catch …
6. Als Jonathan das Boot gerade gekauft hatte, hatte Marissa gehofft, dass er bald
   das Interesse daran verlieren würde.
   … Marissa thought his interest in it would flag …
7. Was Boote für Neuengland waren, waren Lieferwagen mit offener Ladefläche für
   die Südstaaten der USA.
   … the New England version of pick-up trucks … in the rural South.

48 **1.** ☐ refused   ☒ decided   ☐ wanted
   Marissa und Dale hatten sich dafür entschieden, in ein Fischrestaurant zu gehen.

2. ☐ heard about   ☒ gone through   ☐ bought
   Marissa hatte in ihrer Ehe mit Jonathan viel durchgemacht.

3. ☒ gone out   ☐ been seen   ☐ talked
   Dale war der erste Mann seit langer Zeit, mit dem Marissa ausging.

49 **1.** ☐F Abgesehen von ihrem Gesicht war Marissas äußere Erscheinung perfekt.
2. ☐T Marissa sah toll aus, auch ihr Gesicht.
3. ☐F Marissa war sogar einmal auf der Titelseite des Katalogs Victoria's Secret
   gewesen.
4. ☐F Sie hoffte, dass sie jemanden kennenlernen würde, der ihr das Reiten und
   Schießen beibringen würde.
5. ☐F Sie hatte als kleines Mädchen reiten und schießen gelernt und hoffte, einem
   echten Cowboy zu begegnen.
6. ☐T Sie hoffte, dass sie jemanden kennenlernen würde, der sowohl ihre
   Cowgirl- als auch ihre akademische Seite mögen würde oder ganz
   einfach alles an ihr.
7. ☐T Marissa saß nicht gerne alleine in einer Bar.
8. ☐F Sie trank immer ein Glas Wein in einer Bar, nachdem sie einkaufen war.

9. F Dale hatte zu ihr gesagt, er würde sie ein paar Stunden nach der Arbeit treffen.

10. T Er hatte gesagt, er würde eine halbe Stunde nach der Arbeit zum Restaurant kommen.

50 Yarmouth was luxurious in comparison to Green Harbor. People in Yarmouth preferred driving big sport utility vehicles and pickup trucks with flower stickers on them. Houses in Green Harbor overlooked the bay but were quite run down. Joseph Bingham was wearing a tan suit when he walked up the driveway of one of the houses of Cedar Estates. He made a phone call to make sure he was at the right address. Then he rang the bell and the door was opened by a woman with very straight hair.

51 **1.** Joseph Bingham claimed he worked for a cable company.
2. He offered to come back another time.
3. The woman didn't realize that her converter boxes had to be reset.
4. Joseph told her she was supposed to get more channels than she did at the moment.
5. Going by the smell she seemed to have been drinking quite a lot of alcohol.

52 **1.** ☐ was about to ☒ was going to ☐ will
Joseph würde sich einen Drink genehmigen, nachdem er diesen Job erledigt hatte.

2. ☐ am going ☐ will be going ☒ will go
Barbara sagte: „Ich gehe nach oben und zeige Ihnen die Kabelbox."

3. ☐ would have stayed ☒ would be staying ☐ will be staying
Barbara erzählte Joseph, dass die Kinder heute bei ihrem Vater übernachten würden.

4. ☐ was going to ☐ will ☒ would be able to
Joseph sagte, dass Barbara morgen mehr Kanäle empfangen würde.

5. ☒ won't fight ☐ won't be fighting ☐ wouldn't be fighting
Joseph dachte sich: „Wenn ich schnell genug bin, wird Barbara nicht kämpfen."

53 **1.** selfish (egoistisch) – Jonathan
2. drunk (betrunken) – Barbara
3. lonely (einsam) – Marissa
4. cold-blooded (kaltblütig) – Joseph alias Dale
5. crazy about boats (verrückt nach Booten) – Jonathan
6. optimistic (optimistisch) – Marissa

54 **1.** to pull down – to tug down
2. gray hair – salt-and pepper hair
3. to open something – to unzip something
4. empty – deserted
6. good-looking couple – handsome pair
7. physically fit – in very good shape
8. a word or phrase that sounds like another word – a pun

55

1. How does Marissa feel?
- F total deprimiert
- T mal gut, mal schlecht
- F glücklich

2. Why did Marissa's grandfather shoot at the snake?
- F um seiner Enkelin das Schießen beizubringen
- T die Schlange wollte Marissas Pferd beißen
- F um anzugeben

3. Was Marissa looking forward to meeting Dale?
- F gar nicht
- F ein bisschen
- T sie war sich unsicher

56

1. to succeed – to fail
2. rarely – often
3. ugly – good-looking
4. to confirm – to cancel
5. to walk away from someone – to walk up to someone
6. disgust – pleasure
7. unnecessary – necessary

57

1. She was getting tipsy because she had been drinking but had forgotten to eat something.
2. When Dale saw that the restaurant was getting empty he suggested going outside.
3. They sat down on a bench where she had been sitting earlier that evening.
4. It was thrilling and comforting sitting next to Dale but also unsettling.
5. They sat on the bench without talking and were huddling against the cold.
6. After picking up the rope he flexed and unwound it.
7. Dale watched the couple on the boat for a while before asking Marissa if the man was Jonathan.

58

1. F Marissa hatte Dale damit beauftragt, ihren Mann und seine Geliebte umzubringen.

2. T Dale würde Marissas Mann umbringen, nachdem seine Geliebte das Boot verlassen hatte.

3. F Dale war sehr diskret und vermied es, offen über seinen Job zu reden.

4. F Marissa hatte ihren Mann lange beobachtet und wusste mit Sicherheit, dass er sie mit einer einzigen Frau betrog.

5. T Die Tatsache, dass Jonathan normalerweise eine Menge Alkohol konsumierte, machte es für Dale leichter, den Mord wie einen Unfall aussehen zu lassen.

Lösungen

6. [F] Dale erzählte Marissa von der Frau, die er am Tag zuvor ermordet hatte.

7. [F] Barbaras Kinder lebten bei ihrem Vater und sahen ihre Mutter nur an einem Wochenende im Monat.

8. [T] Barbaras Kinder taten Melissa leid.

59

1.	pretty	[X] ziemlich		[X] hübsch		☐ dumm	
2.	current	☐ Währung		[X] Strömung		[X] aktuell	
3.	picture	[X] sich vorstellen		[X] Bild		☐ Krug	
4.	book	[X] reservieren		☐ backen		[X] Buch	
5.	trunk	[X] Rüssel		[X] Kofferraum		☐ Getränk	
6.	table	[X] Tabelle		[X] Tisch		☐ Etikett	
7.	kind	☐ Kind		[X] Art		[X] freundlich	
8.	boot	[X] Computer hochfahren		☐ Boot		[X] Stiefel	

60 Marissa was not quite sure whether she wanted Dale to go ahead and kill her husband. Dale told her he would make sure that everything would work out. Jonathan had given Marissa a hard time because she couldn't have children. Also he had cheated on her numerous times. These and other reasons had driven Marissa to hire Dale and to pay his fee of twenty thousand dollars. She found Dale very attractive but realized there was no future for them.

Wörterverzeichnis

to abuse someone jemanden missbrauchen
accessory Zubehör
ad Anzeige
alimony Unterhaltszahlungen
to amass something etwas anhäufen
to amble over herüberschlendern
anchor line Ankertau
ankle Knöchel
anniversary celebration Hochzeitstagsfeier
to antagonize someone jemanden provozieren
to associate someone with someone jemanden mit jemandem in Verbindung bringen
attaché case Aktenkoffer
at the top of the landing oben am Treppenabsatz

balding schütter werdend
barbed wire Stacheldraht
to be (was – were) about to do something im Begriff sein, etwas zu tun
to be accustomed to something an etwas gewöhnt sein
to be a dime a dozen wie Sand am Meer vorhanden sein
to be antagonistic towards someone sich jemandem gegenüber feindselig verhalten
to be a sight kein schöner Anblick sein
bedraggled ungepflegt
bedspread Tagesdecke
to be five-five 1,62 cm groß sein
to be frantic verzweifelt sein
to be going to werden
to be in season Saison haben
to be into something auf etwas stehen
to be kidding Scherze machen
benefit Benefizveranstaltung
to be nuts verrückt sein
to be patronizing to someone jemanden von oben herab behandeln
to be reminiscent of someone an jemanden erinnern
to be scared Angst haben
to be stifled erstickt werden
to be studded with something voll von etwas sein
to be tucked (away) versteckt liegen
bewildered verwirrt
billowy schwadenartig
blackberry Brombeere
to blackmail someone jemanden erpressen
bleak trostlos
bloody mess blutige Masse

Wörterverzeichnis **125**

blunt stumpf
bluntly geradeheraus
to bob hin und her schwanken
bod Körper
boldly mutig
boob Busen
borderline im Grenzbereich
to bound hoppeln
branch office Zweigstelle
brass Messing
brush Unterholz
built-in Einbau-
to bump something gegen etwas
  stoßen
bumper sticker Aufkleber
bunch Haufen
buoy Boje
business associate Geschäftspartner
butt Hintern
by my little old lonesome ganz
  alleine

C

cackle Gackern
call Entscheidung
can Dose
to cancel absagen
candlelit mit Kerzen beleuchtet
carpenter Zimmermann
to cart something back etwas nach
  Hause/zurück schleppen
caseload Fälle
cash Bargeld
casually lässig
catch Fang
certified cheque gedeckter Scheck
to charge someone something jemandem etwas berechnen

to charm someone sich bei jemandem einschmeicheln
to chase someone down jemanden
  aufspüren
to check untersuchen
to check up on someone jemandem
  nachspionieren
cheerfully fröhlich
chill Frösteln
china Porzellan
to choke something etwas unter-
  drücken
to chuck something etwas hin-
  schmeißen
church choir director Kirchenchor-
  leiter(in)
to cinch something for someone jemandem etwas glasklar machen
to claim something etwas behaupten
cleanser Reinigungsmittel
clerk Verkäufer(in)
clinging klammernd
to clear one's throat sich räuspern
to clink one's glass to someone
  else's mit jemandem anstoßen
clip Ladestreifen
clue Hinweis, Spur
cluster Gruppe
clutch Kupplung
to clutch something etwas um-
  klammert halten
to cock one's head seinen Kopf auf
  die Seite legen
to cock something etwas spannen
to coddle someone jemanden
  umsorgen
cod dockhand Dockhelfer(in) beim
  Kabeljaufang

to coil sich zusammenringeln

to come (came – come) to do something anfangen etwas zu tun

comforting beruhigend

to commit someone jemanden in eine Anstalt einweisen

compact Puderdose

compulsive zwanghaft

confidential vertraulich

confidentiality Schweigepflicht

configuration Aufbau

to consume something etwas beherrschen

to cook something up etwas kochen

co-op Apartment

countertransference Gegenübertragung

cover Titelseite

coveralls Overalls

to cover something für etwas zuständig sein

to cover something up etwas verbergen

cover to cover von Anfang bis Ende

crab Krabbe

to crack versagen

to crackle to life knisternd angehen

to cradle something etwas festhalten

to crank something down etwas herunterkurbeln

to cross something über etwas gehen

to crouch kauern

to cruise gemütlich fahren

cruising altitude Reiseflughöhe

cuff Manschette

current aktuell

cute süß

D

to dab at something etwas betupfen

daisy Gänseblümchen

damn: He doesn't give a damn. Es ist ihm scheißegal.

to debate überlegen

decent anständig

delusional wahnsinnig

to delve into something sich in etwas vertiefen

den Arbeitszimmer

to deny something etwas abstreiten

deserted menschenleer

developmental and IQ issue Frage der Entwicklung und Intelligenz

discarded weggeworfen

discontented unzufrieden

disgusted angewidert

disheveled unordentlich

dismay Bestürzung

to dismount absteigen

disposal of evidence Beseitigung von Beweismaterial

dive Spelunke

to divorce someone sich von jemandem scheiden lassen

Doesn't fly. Das zieht nicht.

to do (did – done) for work beruflich machen

to do impersonations Stimmen nachahmen

to do straps die Riemen zumachen

to double-check something etwas noch einmal überprüfen

down to the nth degree bis ins kleinste Detail

downward spiral Abwärtsspirale

Wörterverzeichnis **127**

to draw (drew – drawn) down herunterziehen
drawl schleppender Akzent
driveway Auffahrt
drowsiness Schläfrigkeit
drug company Pharmaunternehmen
dry dock Trockendock
to dump someone jemanden fallen lassen
dutifully pflichtbewusst

edge Schärfe
embarrassed peinlich berührt
evenly gelassen
evergreen Nadelbaum
evidence Beweis
excruciating unvorstellbar hoch
exhilarated euphorisch
expert witness fee Sachverständigenhonorar
to exude something etwas ausströmen

F-150 Ford Pick-up
to fade verebben
to fake something etwas vortäuschen
to favor someone jemanden bevorzugen
to figure something out sich etwas ausrechnen
fingerprint Fingerabdruck
to finish something etwas austrinken
firefly Leuchtkäfer

to fire up the engine den Motor anlassen
fishing and packing town Fischerei- und Verpackungsstadt
fishy zweifelhaft
to fix something etwas in Ordnung bringen
to flag abflauen
to flail um sich schlagen
to flare aufflackern
to flex something etwas biegen
flight attendant Steward, Stewardess
flustered durcheinander
to fly (flew – flown) into a rage einen Wutanfall bekommen
folder Mappe
foot Fuß
for als
to forge something etwas fälschen
-framed glasses Brille mit … -Gestell
to freeze (froze – frozen) erstarren
frizzy kraus
frown Stirnrunzeln
to frown die Stirn runzeln
frozen mit versteinerter Miene
full scholarship Vollstipendium
fun verrückt
funny komisch
fuzzy kraus

garbage Mist
garrotte Garrotte (Würgeisen)
to gasp something etwas hervorstoßen
to get (got – got) ahead Karriere machen

to get away with something mit etwas ungestraft davonkommen
to get beat up zusammengeschlagen werden
to get engaged sich verloben
to get off doing something sich etwas anmaßen
to get out of something sich vor etwas drücken
to get tangled in something sich in etwas verfangen
to get tipsy langsam beschwipst werden
to get to the bottom of something etwas auf den Grund gehen
given angesichts
glossy glänzend
GPS system Navigationssystem
to graduate from a medical school etc. seinen Abschluss an einer medizinischen Hochschule etc. machen
gravely ernst
grieving trauernd
to grind one's teeth together mit den Zähnen knirschen
grip Halt; Händedruck
groggily benommen
gross ekelhaft
to grow (grew – grown) werden
gruff barsch

half-ton Halbtonner
to handle something mit etwas klarkommen; etwas angehen
hardly kaum
harsh scharf

haunch Hinterlauf
to have (had – had) resentment toward someone für jemanden negative Gefühle haben
hazily wie durch einen Schleier
hazy trüb
to head gehen
head-on direkt
heirloom Erbstück
hemlock Hemlock-Tanne
to hesitate zögern
high-rise Hochhaus
hit-man protocol Killer-Spielregeln
to hit (hit – hit) someone jemanden überfallen
honk Hupen
to hospitalize someone jemanden ins Krankenhaus einweisen
housekeeper Haushälterin
to huddle sich zusammenkauern
to hug someone jemanden umarmen
to hunt jagen

to idle im Leerlauf sein
impeccable makellos
to impersonate someone jemanden imitieren
impromptu session Spontansitzung
in a flash auf der Stelle
inch Inch
in droves in Scharen
inexact ungenau
in-flight magazine Bordmagazin
insanity Unzurechnungsfähigkeit
instantaneous sofort
insurance claim Versicherungsschadensanspruch

Wörterverzeichnis

internship praktisches Jahr
investment account Anlagekonto
involuntary commitment Zwangseinweisung
irritated gereizt
issue Thema

jailor Gefängnisbeamter, -beamtin
to jam something etwas einklemmen
joint custody gemeinsames Sorgerecht
juxtaposition Nebeneinanderstellung

to keep (kept – kept) a diary of something über etwas Tagebuch führen
to keep one's wits about one einen klaren Kopf behalten
to keep someone pinned down jemanden niederhalten
key chain Schlüsselanhänger
to kick someone out jemanden rauswerfen
knapsack Rucksack

lack of Mangel an
latch Verschluss
lately in letzter Zeit
latest neueste
law enforcement rule Gesetzesregel
lead defense lawyer Hauptverteidiger(in)
lean hager
to leap (leapt – leapt) springen

leather interior Ledersitze
lecturing professor Professor(in), der/die eine Vorlesung hält
legacy Erbe
legitimate in Ordnung
lessee (= let's see) mal sehen
leverage Hebelkraft
to lift verfliegen
light Ampel
lightning bug Leuchtkäfer
liquor Alkohol
little ein bisschen
lobster trap Hummerfalle
log Baumstamm
to look someone over jemanden mustern
lop-eared mit Hängeohren
lot Parkplatz
to lounge es sich bequem machen

M

to make (made – made) a mess eine Schweinerei machen
to make an issue of something etwas aufbauschen
to make a stink about something wegen etwas Ärger machen
mall Einkaufszentrum
mandatory rehearing vorgeschriebene Wiederanhörung
mantra Mantra
maple leaves Ahornblätter
marble marmorn
marine engine treatment Wartung von Schiffsmotoren
massage parlor Massagesalon
matron Matrone
matted verfilzt

medical examiner Gerichtsmediziner(in)
to memorize something etwas auswendig lernen
mental case Mensch mit schweren seelischen Störungen
mildly leicht
mimic Imitator(in)
mph (= miles per hour) Meilen pro Stunde
mug Becher
murder in the first degree Mord
mystified verblüfft

to nag someone into doing something jemandem die Hölle heiß machen, bis er/sie etwas tut
name tag Namensschild
natural-born geborene(r)
naw nein
necessities notwendige Dinge
negligent homicide fahrlässiger Totschlag
nope nein
not a soul keine Menschenseele
numb wie betäubt
nursery Gärtnerei
nut case jemand, der ziemlich verrückt ist

oak leaves Eichenblätter
occupant Bewohner(in)
offhand beiläufig geäußert
office manager Büroleiter(in)
on blocks aufgebockt
on the brink auf der Kippe

to originate in something in etwas seinen Ursprung haben
to overhear (overheard – overheard) something etwas zufällig mitbekommen
overmedication Einnahme zu vieler Medikamente

to pace auf und ab gehen
to paint the town die Stadt unsicher machen
palm Handfläche
to pamper someone jemanden verwöhnen
to pass out in Ohnmacht fallen
patch Fleck
pelt Pelz
penthouse triplex Penthousewohnung über drei Etagen
pest Nervensäge
petite zierlich
to pick someone up jemanden abschleppen
to pick something etwas aussuchen
pile Haufen
pine Kiefer
Pinot Noir by the glass offener Pinot Noir
pitiful mitleiderregend
pity schade
pleased zufrieden
plebeian plebejisch
to plummet stürzen
to point at zielen auf
poorly-lit schlecht beleuchtet
porch Veranda
portfolio Anlagevermögen

Wörterverzeichnis

Post-it note Haftnotiz
to post something etwas einzäunen
premeditated vorsätzlich
prenuptial agreement Ehevertrag
preoccupied konzentriert
prerequisite Grundvoraussetzung
to press something etwas bügeln
to pretend so tun als ob
private eye Privatdetektiv(in)
to protrude from something aus etwas hängen
to prove beweisen
pudgy schwammig
to pull off the road anhalten
pun Wortspiel
puppy Welpe
purse Handtasche
to pursue something einer Sache nachgehen
to put (put – put) someone on a tube jemandem eine Magensonde legen
to put something aside etwas vergessen

to question something etwas infrage stellen
to quit aufhören
quitting time Feierabend
quizzical fragend

raft Floß
to raise a stink Stunk machen
to ramble on and on ohne Ende quasseln
rambling weitschweifig
rapist Vergewaltiger

real-life wahr
reams of tief
rear deck Achterdeck
rearview-mirror test Rückspiegeltest
reasonably in ruhigem Ton
to recall sich erinnern
rectangle Rechteck
to redeem something etwas retten
regimen strenges Regiment
regulars list Gästeliste
reluctantly widerwillig
remote Fernbedienung
to reschedule einen anderen Termin machen
to research recherchieren
resolution Vorsatz
retail therapy Shopping-Therapie
rhinoplasty Nasenkorrektur
to rig something up etwas installieren
to roar rauschen
robin Rotkehlchen
to rummage in something in etwas wühlen
run Laufmasche
rung Sprosse
to run (ran – run) up debts Schulden machen
rural ländlich
rusting rostend

safety Sicherung
salt-and-pepper grau meliert
sane gesund
to scan something etwas mit den Augen absuchen

scent Geruch

to screw something up etwas ver-
masseln

to seal something etwas zukleben

sentenced verurteilt

services rendered geleistete Dienste

session Sitzung

set Fernseher

to set (set – set) someone up jemandem etwas anhängen

to settle on something sich für etwas entscheiden

severe schwer

shack Hütte

shade Rollo

shallow oberflächlich

shard Scherbe

sharp kühl

to shift schweifen

shingle Schild

shot Schütze, Schützin

shower Party

to shred something etwas zerrupfen

shrink Seelenklempner(in)

to shrug mit den Schultern zucken

shrunken eingesunken

sidewalk Gehweg

to sift through something etwas
durchblättern

sight (seltsamer) Anblick

to sight down on something auf etwas richten

to sip something an etwas nippen

to size someone up jemanden ab-
schätzen

skintight hauteng

skirt Saum

skull Schädel

slab Scheibe

slacks Hose

to slam something shut etwas zu-
knallen

sleek gepflegt

slick-slimy schlüpfrig-schleimig

to slip into something in etwas ver-
fallen

to slip to something zu etwas wan-
dern

sloppy schlampig

slut nurse Krankenschwester-
Schlampe

to smash the hell out of something
etwas mit aller Kraft zertrümmern

to smear one's face with something
sich etwas ins Gesicht schmieren

to snag something etwas heraus-
zupfen

to snap jemanden anfahren

snappy zackig

to sneak up sich heranschleichen

to sniff something an etwas schnup-
pern

snotty arrogant

sob Schluchzen

to sob schluchzen

soda can Getränkedose

sole einzig

to spank someone jemanden ver-
sohlen

sparrow Spatz

speaker Lautsprecher

specifics Einzelheiten

to speed rasen

spicy würzig

Wörterverzeichnis 133

to spin sich drehen
spirits Stimmung
split-level mit versetzten Geschossen
to split (split – split) up sich trennen
to spoil someone jemanden verwöhnen
to sport something mit etwas protzen
spotlight Scheinwerfer
to sprain something sich etwas verstauchen
spritely schnittig
squat nichts
to squeeze something off etwas abdrücken
stacked aufgestapelt
to stall stehen bleiben
standard procedure Normalfall
stately würdevoll
state trooper Staatspolizist(in)
to stay in control sich unter Kontrolle halten
to steer through something durch etwas steuern
stern Heck; streng
sternly ernsthaft
stodgy nichtssagend
stoplight Ampel
to straddle something rittlings auf etwas sitzen
straight pur
straightjacket Zwangsjacke
strand Litze
streak Streifen
to strike (struck – struck) someone hard jemandem einen ziemlichen Schlag versetzen

to strike something auf etwas aufschlagen
stringy strähnig
to study something sich etwas genauer anschauen
to summarize zusammenfassen
supple weich
to support oneself on something sich an etwas abstützen
to surrender to something etwas nachgeben
suspicious misstrauisch
to sway in something sich in etwas wiegen
to swell sich bilden

T

tan hellbraun
teaching hospital Lehrkrankenhaus
tea kettle Wasserkessel
tenacious hartnäckig
to testify aussagen
the hell with zur Hölle mit
There you go. Na bitte.
thigh Oberschenkel
thrilling erregend
thud Satz
to thud pochen
timbre Timbre
time-consuming zeitraubend
tons of massenweise
tool of the trade Arbeitsmaterial
to toss something etwas werfen
townhouse Reihenhaus
trace evidence Spuren
trail Wanderweg
transference Übertragung
transmission Getriebe

trash bin Mülleimer
tree line Baumgrenze
trigger auslösend
trim gepflegt
trust Stiftung
tryst Schäferstündchen
to tug something down etwas herunterziehen
to turn one's back on someone jemandem den Rücken zudrehen
twist Wendung
twisted length verdrehtes Stück

unaccompanied-minor form Formular für alleinreisende Kinder
to undo (undid – undone) something etwas aufknöpfen
uneasily unbehaglich
unsettling beunruhigend
to unwind (unwound – unwound) something etwas entwirren
to unzip something den Reißverschluss von etwas öffnen
upscale vornehm
upturned nose Stupsnase
used: he used to do something er hat früher etwas gemacht
utterly völlig

vasectomy Sterilisation
vessel Schiff
to victimize someone jemanden ungerecht behandeln
virtually fast
to volunteer ehrenamtlich helfen

to walk single file im Gänsemarsch gehen
walk-up Wohnung ohne Aufzug
to waltz around herumtun
warily misstrauisch
waterfront Hafen
watershed event Wendepunkt
way to go alle Achtung
weird seltsam
wharf Kai
when it comes to … wenn es um … geht
to whine about something über etwas jammern
willow switch Weidenrute
to wince zusammenzucken
windbreaker Windjacke
to wipe something etwas abwischen
with flying colors mit Bravour
to withdraw (withdrew – withdrawn) sich zurückziehen
to work out trainieren
to wrestle with something mit etwas ringen
wrinkled zerknittert
wryly ironisch

yep ja
you bet und ob
youngster Kind

Englisch lernen Berlitz®
mit Nervenkitzel

Mit den spannenden englischen Kurzkrimis der renommierten Autoren Jeffery Deaver und Ian Rankin ist Lesespaß garantiert.
Kurze, überschaubare Originaltexte, hilfreiche Vokabelerklärungen und Übungen machen das Englischlernen zum kurzweiligen Zeitvertreib!

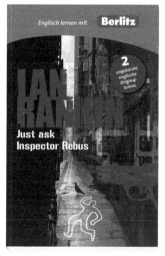

Berlitz
Englisch lernen mit Ian Rankin
Just ask Inspector Rebus

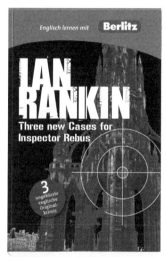

Berlitz
Englisch lernen mit Ian Rankin
Three new Cases for Inspector Rebus

Infos & mehr
www.berlitzpublishing.de

Vom Anfänger zum Superhero

„Heldenhaftes Englisch" mit Superman und Batman garantieren die neuen Berlitz Comic-Lektüren. Dank der Ausklappseiten mit Vokabelerklärungen und der Comic-Bilder können bereits fortgeschrittene Anfänger den englischen Originaltext leicht verstehen und beim entspannten Comic-Schmökern ihre Sprachkenntnisse verbessern.

Berlitz
Englisch lernen mit Superman
Up, up and away!

Berlitz
Englisch lernen mit Batman
Bad Guys Gallery

SUPERMAN and BATMAN and all related names, characters and elements are trademarks of DC Comics © 2007. All Rights Reserved

Infos & mehr
www.berlitzpublishing.de